Practical Preservation and Conservation Strategies for Libraries

Practical Preservation and Conservation Strategies for Libraries

Brian J. Baird

Illustrated by Jody Brown

ROWMAN & LITTLEFIELD
Lanham • Boulder • New York • London

Published by Rowman & Littlefield
An imprint of The Rowman & Littlefield Publishing Group, Inc.
4501 Forbes Boulevard, Suite 200, Lanham, Maryland 20706
www.rowman.com

Unit A, Whitacre Mews, 26-34 Stannary Street, London SE11 4AB

British Library Cataloguing in Publication Information Available

Library of Congress Cataloging-in-Publication Data Available

ISBN 978-1-5381-0958-8 (hardback : alk. paper) | ISBN 978-1-5381-0959-5 (pbk. : alk.
paper) | ISBN 978-1-5381-0960-1 (ebook)

♾™ The paper used in this publication meets the minimum requirements of American
National Standard for Information Sciences—Permanence of Paper for Printed Library
Materials, ANSI/NISO Z39.48-1992.

Printed in the United States of America

To my seven children,
Zachariah, Madeline, Miriam, Amanda, Joseph, Tatiana, and Natalie,
who have all developed a strong love of books
and the long-term value they hold.

Contents

Figures and Tables

Figures

Table

Foreword

The preservation and conservation of published materials, both monographs and periodicals, has primarily been an invisible operation to the reading public. While not all libraries can afford to hire specialized staff or operate conservation labs, most practitioners would agree that preservation work is an important aspect of librarianship and an essential part of maintaining healthy collections. The advent of digital publishing has made the library preservation issue more complex as new formats are used together with the traditional codex. Along with physical materials, bits and bytes must now be preserved to maintain the integrity of the written word.

The digital publishing age gave rise to the hope that library preservation operations could be simplified and streamlined. Indeed, thanks to electronic resources, some aspects of preservation have been simplified. One only has to look at the reduction in most libraries' binding budgets over the past decade to see this trend in action: as more serials are available electronically, the physical copies are not retained. But unfortunately, binding is only one small aspect of collection preservation. As digital humanities and digital scholarship becomes more prevalent, all libraries, including public, academic, research, and specialized, have to contend with the challenges of preserving born-digital materials along with maintaining their physical collections.

Physical collections remain relevant because contrary to a popular belief by some that all information is available online and e-readers have replaced the book, the fact is that most people still prefer reading physical books to the electronic version. According to a recent Pew Research Center study, "fully 65% of Americans have read a print book in the last year, more than double the share that has read an e-book (28%) and more than four times the share that has consumed book content via audio book (14%)."[1] So while more publications, particularly scholarly, are available digitally, there remains a demand for more traditional formats from the reading public. While different, all these formats have preservation and conservation needs. The one constant between all these formats is that if we hope to maintain these publications for future generations, we cannot ignore their preservation needs.

Practical Preservation and Conservation Strategies for Libraries provides an excellent overview of the complex challenges that all libraries now face in the preservation of the various publishing formats. It provides insights to work that should be done in-house as well as preservation approaches best outsourced or undertaken collaboratively. But this book provides more than just a summary of conservation strategies; it can also be used as a guide for establishing a preservation program in academic and public libraries. *Practical Preservation and Conservation Strategies for Libraries* is essential reading for anyone concerned about the challenges libraries face in the care for library collections, both print and digital.

Bradley L. Schaffner
college librarian
Carleton College, Northfield, Minnesota
bschaffner@carleton.edu

Note

1. Pew Research Center, "Book Reading 2016," September 2016, accessed July 20, 2017, http://www.pewinternet.org.

Preface

Preservation efforts in small academic and public libraries are often a difficult challenge due to the constant obstacles of limited funding, insufficient staffing, and lack of expertise. These challenges are made more difficult in the digital age where how libraries acquire and lend information has changed dramatically. This book addresses the dynamic environment libraries face in the electronic age and how these changes impact their preservation efforts.

Librarianship is about managing resources. And at the end of the day, after the library is staffed; materials are acquired, processed, and made available to patrons; and the light bill is paid, there is little funding left for preservation or much else. For this reason the preservation strategies presented here are designed to reduce immediate and long-term costs, and strengthen the library's collection-development goals.

The first step, when beginning a preservation program, is to clearly document the preservation needs of the library. A proper analysis involves establishing use patterns for the collections, thoroughly evaluating the collection-development plan, assessing the potential threats to the materials held, and identifying the preservation resources readily available. In the following pages several preservation strategies are presented. The application of these strategies will be different for each library, but their use will result in a strong, library-wide, preservation plan for acquiring, processing, and circulating the library collections.

By using an assessment-based approach, a library can develop a preservation strategy created to best meet its specific needs. This approach will allow a library to identify its preservation concerns and challenges, thus providing a clear indication of what the library should do over time to improve its preservation efforts.

Preservation efforts are most effective when they take a pragmatic approach. Few libraries can afford to have ideal preservation programs that fully address the needs of their collections. Therefore, this manual is designed to help libraries learn to identify areas of concern, optimize the use of resources put toward preservation, and establish goals for continual improvement over time as additional resources come available.

This book is designed as a general overview to educate people interested in library preservation, and as a "how to" manual to provide libraries with practical information to help them grapple with specific preservation challenges. Because the strategies in this volume are practical-based information, the book reflects the major paradigm shifts that have taken place in libraries and information management in the twenty-first century.

The book will first outline strategies for paper-based collections. It will then discuss digital preservation. Digital preservation is very important and will become increasingly important with each passing year, but it is presented as the last chapter in this book because the general principles and strategies discussed in the earlier chapters will provide important context for establishing a digital-preservation strategy for your library.

Acknowledgments

I would like to thank Jody Brown for his exceptional illustrations that add so much to the text. I also appreciate all of the libraries and wonderful library staffs I have worked so closely with over the years as a librarian, conservator, and service provider. Together, we have developed some wonderful preservation strategies and practical solutions to rather challenging problems.

Chapter 1

Crossing the Preservation Rubicon

In 49 BCE Julius Caesar made a conscious decision to break a long-standing, sacrosanct Roman law. He broke with tradition that was nearly as old as the republic itself. He crossed the River Rubicon into Rome with his troops. From this historic event the phrase "crossing the Rubicon" has come to mean a significant sea change, or major shift in policy or practice. Library preservation came of age in the late twentieth century as a result of strong leadership in the field of librarianship and a shared commitment to create national preservation endeavors and standards. This strong leadership and energy has carried preservation practices into the twenty-first century but has also resulted in an inertia where practices have remained largely unchanged in spite of the rapidly changing nature of scholarly communication.

In the twenty-first century information comes to us in many formats—as it always has, but now the vast majority of scholarly information is electronic. As a result, library preservation must cross the Rubicon and become primarily digital preservation. It is important to understand that there will *always* be a need for traditional practices of preserving print format materials, reformatting, disaster planning, and optimizing the environmental conditions in our libraries. But rather than describing the entire scope of preservation, these efforts are now only a subset of our preservation responsibilities. But the good news is that it has become easier than ever to share preservation efforts across multiple libraries and organizations.

The challenge of digital preservation is immense and grows larger every year as more and more information is made available in various electronic forms. But it is not just a matter of volume; it is also a matter of ever-changing formats, improved delivery and storage systems, and the complexity of the information being presented. In the past, preservation was a passive, benign activity. In the latter part of the twentieth century libraries became alarmed by the problem of brittle, acidic paper in collections across the country. The brittle-books problem presented a huge threat to the future of scholarship, but a book printed on very acidic, weak paper stored in less than optimal conditions will still last many decades. Acidic paper is bad, but it does not result in the immediate destruction of the object. That is not true for digital information. Unless proactive efforts are made to preserve a digital file and migrate it regularly to the latest version of the presentation software, the file can become unusable in a matter of a few years. Put another way, in the past, when totalitarian regimes wanted to destroy information they found offensive, they had to round up these publications and burn them. This required a concerted, proactive effort to achieve the goal, and even then it was rarely successful as a government could seldom destroy all copies of an offending title. But now, when important digital information is stored centrally by vendors and publishers, there is the distinct possibility that publications could be lost in the blink of an eye. This means librarianship must make a concerted, proactive effort to preserve digital information or it will be lost.

What does contemporary and future library preservation look like on the south side of the preservation Rubicon? How does the electronic information age shift the preservation paradigm? Every library is unique, but in general terms what follows is how twenty-first century library preservation needs to operate. This chapter will provide a general overview of library preservation in the future. Following chapters will build on the foundational principles outlined below. This book outlines strategies for preservation of paper-based and electronic information for small academic and public libraries that do not have preservation professionals on staff.

Cooperation

Effective digital preservation will require cooperation. Every library has its unique digital collections that it needs to preserve. That means local institutions need to address issues such as organizing, storing, and migrating these collections forward to new platforms over time. This is an area that is ripe for robust collaboration to help one another. The LOCKSS (Lots of Copies Keeps Stuff Safe) program is just one of many examples of how this can work. In the analog age, preservation was largely an individual library issue; digital preservation goes beyond the walls of the library and is impacted by technology decisions made at administrative levels above the library or by publishers. For resources purchased, or leased, from a vendor (which are most of them) only preservation efforts made at a consortial or national level will ensure this information will survive. Publishers have a vested interest in preserving the information they want to sell to their library clients, but as the volume of information continues to grow exponentially, and as older material gets accessed less and less often, the temptation will be to shed the less used (and less profitable) information.

There are some good models and practices in place for cooperative digital preservation (e.g., HathiTrust), but more resources need to be directed toward this effort. Collaborative efforts have always been a key part of librarianship and preservation, but it is even more vital in the twenty-first century.

Libraries will continue to hold books and serials. But as more and more libraries search their buildings to find space for new or expanding public services, care must be taken in how physical collections are reduced. Collection management projects should include cooperation between libraries to ensure that a strong shared collection is maintained by the combined efforts of multiple libraries.

Environmental Conditions

Ensuring that library collections are stored in consistently maintained environments with carefully controlled temperatures and relative humidity has been a standard preservation practice for generations. These efforts should continue, but increasingly there are pressures from global environmental concerns to reduce the amount of energy used to heat and cool libraries. This will be an issue libraries will continue to grapple with over the coming decades. The optimum conditions for storing paper-based collections are different than those for storing electronic information. Libraries will always have their special collections and archives that they will want to hold forever, and storing them in optimal environmental conditions is paramount, but in an electronic information age, the long-term storage of general collections should be reexamined at both the national and individual library level (see below for more on this).

Disaster Planning

Many would argue that professional library preservation got its birth as a result of disaster recovery efforts following the Florence, Italy, flood in 1966. Traditionally, disaster plans were designed to help prevent disasters and to cope with them proactively when they did occur, thus preserving the vast majority of the library's collections. But in the twenty-first century, if a university or city lost its library in a major disaster, would they rebuild their library and its collections the same as it was before—even if money was not an issue? In the twenty-first century a library's disaster plan should start with the institutions IT disaster plan and build off that as needed to address its specific needs.

Physical Treatment

Conservation treatment and commercial binding have always been key components to library preservation. They will remain important, but in the twenty-first century conservation should be handled in a consortial arrangement where multiple institutions share the significant costs of building, staffing, and supplying conservation facilities. Library binding has always been one of the most efficient and cost-effective preservation activities. It still is, but far less binding needs to be done. Gone are the days of much of the proactive binding. Materials should only be bound when they are damaged, or when they are too fragile to hold up to library use. Libraries have dramatically cut their binding budgets over the past decade, but most are still binding too many items out of habit rather than as a result of a thoughtful preservation plan.

Reformatting

Microfilming was a bedrock preservation activity for decades and serves as a good model for digital reformatting efforts today. Many reformatting projects were grant funded, and efforts were made to ensure these projects both preserved *and* increased access to that information and that efforts were not duplicated. Reformatting was the original cooperative preservation effort and should be the model for nearly all preservation efforts today. As will be discussed, not all digitization is preservation, but all digital-preservation efforts will eventually involve some form of reformatting as files are migrated forward to new presentation platforms and storage technologies.

Repositories

Ideally, across the country, there would be three to five regional repositories for print materials to ensure multiple copies of every title are preserved and made available through interlibrary loan or digital delivery. Doing this on a national level would make sure these repository collections are complete, well preserved, and sharable, and will help minimize duplication of efforts. These efforts could also promote efficiency and cost-effectiveness in preserving print collections. Print collections stored under good environmental conditions is still a very effective strategy for the long-term preservation of information, and conducting these efforts as part of a national program makes sense on several levels. Existing large, consortial storage facilities that are shared by multiple institutions demonstrate how effective this model can be. The same model could be used for digital preservation by expanding on several of the consortial digital-preservation efforts already in use.

In conclusion, preservation in the twenty-first century *must* be proactive and conducted at a level beyond the walls of the library. If not, vast amounts of information could be lost. The Rubicon has been crossed. The only question is, will we have a plan for efficiently and effectively moving to Rome?

Chapter 2

Environmental Conditions

We begin with environmental conditions because controlling the temperature and relative humidity in a library is the most important effort a library can undertake to preserve its collections. Controlling the temperature and relative humidity are important because the environment impacts every item in the collection every minute of every day. Thus, if the environmental conditions are good, years of useful life are added to materials in the collection, and if the conditions are bad, years of life are continually drained from each and every item.

As a general rule, colder is better for library materials of all types. However, because people also occupy libraries, their comfort must be considered. A general rule of thumb is to constantly keep the temperature as close to seventy degrees Fahrenheit as possible with a relative humidity between 35 and 50 percent.

The reason for controlling the temperature and relative humidity is twofold. First, there is the acidic paper problem. Beginning in about 1850, papermakers began using wood fiber to produce their paper. Wood fiber makes strong, consistent paper, but it requires harsh chemicals to break the wood down into fibers suitable to produce paper. As a result, residual chemicals remain in the paper after it is produced. Until the 1980s, most paper produced in the world contained harsh acids that were left in the paper causing it to become weak and brittle over time. Acidic papers break down by turning yellow or brown as the acids in the paper destroy the fibers, causing them to become weak and fragile. Paper can become so brittle and weak that it will literally crumble to dust in your hand when you try to bend it. Heat and moisture act as catalysts in paper to increase the rate of paper degradation. For this reason, if a library is kept relatively cool and dry, the paper will last much longer. For example, research has shown that keeping a library at sixty-seven degrees and 40 percent relative humidity instead of seventy-two degrees and 50 percent humidity can extend the life of a collection by as much as 40 percent![1]

In addition to avoiding high temperature and relative humidity, it is also important to maintain constant environmental levels in the library when possible. Many experts call for a temperature of seventy degrees plus or minus two degrees and a relative humidity of 50 percent plus or minus 5 percent. This can present a real challenge for many libraries. Very few buildings have the heating, ventilation, and air-conditioning (HVAC) systems, or necessary insulation, to maintain a constant temperature and relative humidity. This is a goal that is unrealistic unless the building has been built specifically to provide this level of control. Therefore, efforts should be made to optimize the conditions in the library. Furthermore, there have been efforts in recent years to reduce the energy consumption in libraries by turning down the HVAC system at night and on days when the library is closed as a way to conserve energy. This is not ideal for collections, but many libraries are less concerned about preserving their paper collections long term since most new information comes into the library in an electronic format. Electronic information and energy conservation are just two more variables to consider when optimizing a library's environment.

Optimizing Library Environment

Optimizing a library's environmental conditions means maintaining the best environment possible for the library. To do this, the first step is to carefully analyze the temperature and relative humidity in the building. Monitor both for several months to determine how they change relative to the outside weather conditions and the seasons. In addition, it is important to carefully evaluate the building itself to determine what impacts the internal environment such as the HVAC system, windows, and the insulation. The easiest way to monitor the temperature and relative humidity in the library is to check what capabilities your HVAC system has. Most new systems will gather temperature and relative humidity data, but usually they will not gather all the information you need. It will probably be necessary to supplement the HVAC data with information gathered using data loggers designed for this purpose. There are several different models on the market ranging in cost from nearly a thousand dollars to less than a hundred dollars each. In choosing a data logger it is important to get a model that will provide accurate readings and give you the memory capabilities you need. Some models provide long-term memory that will record data for several months at a time. Other models require you to take more frequent readings. High-end models allow you to gather the data in real time via a wireless connection.

The number of data loggers needed is determined by the layout of the library. A library that covers several floors and several rooms will need more data loggers than a library on one floor with large, open spaces. Sunlight heating part of the library, drafty areas, and how well the HVAC system works all effect the environment of the library. Placing data loggers throughout the library will enable you to determine what is happening with the temperature and relative humidity in each location over time. By moving the data loggers around the building you will learn where to place the units to get the most accurate readings possible. For example, Watson Library at the University of Kansas is made up of three stack areas that were built onto the main building in various remodeling projects. We began monitoring the collections in Watson with many data loggers, moving them around every few months to determine how, or if, the environment differed on various floors of the various stack areas. In time, we learned that we could use five data loggers to effectively monitor the entire building. This freed up data loggers to be used to monitor other libraries around campus.

When distributing the data loggers throughout the building, it will be important to place a few in the stack areas to determine what is happening where materials are stored. Placing a data logger on a shelf near a window where it might be subject to a draft or direct sunlight will skew the results of your data. Likewise, placing a data logger near the ceiling or near the floor will affect the results you obtain.

It will be important to monitor the temperature and relative humidity for several months—especially if you live in a location that has seasonal changes. In such locations it will be especially important to monitor the environment during the spring and fall when the outside temperatures are most erratic. In addition to monitoring the temperature and relative humidity inside the library, it is wise to also collect data on the weather patterns outside the library. It will be helpful in analyzing swings or variations in temperature and relative humidity in the library if you have data on what is happening outside. For example, you can expect to see higher humidity in the library when it is raining outside and lower humidity in the building during dry, hot periods outside.

In addition to monitoring the environment, it will also be important to learn about the HVAC system used in your library. Learn how it works, who controls it, the strengths and weakness of the system, and what controls you have over the system. Generally, the first step to learning this information is a conversation with the person in charge of facilities for the building. This might be a library employee, or it may be a city or college employee. These people often have a wealth of information about the building and can be a great asset in helping you optimize the environment in your library. Their expertise will also prove helpful in disaster planning (see chapter 10 on disaster planning). Explain to the facilities person your concerns for the collections and why it is important to have well-controlled environmental conditions. This will enable him or her to help optimize the library's environment.

After you have monitored the library's temperature and relative humidity for three or four seasons, and have collected enough data to identify patterns in how various parts of your library react to outside weather conditions and seasonal changes, you can begin working with your facilities personnel to find ways to optimize the environmental conditions in the library. Some fixes are relatively easy. Often simple things such as portable dehumidification equipment, or recalibrating the thermostats in the library, can have large positive effects. Blinds or shades can also have a large impact by blocking the sun from shining into the building and overheating it. Likewise, effective use of weather stripping and window sealants can help reduce unwanted air exchange. The important thing is to identify the easy wins and to take advantage of them. Through careful monitoring and close cooperation with the facilities personnel responsible for the library, most libraries can easily improve their environmental conditions with relatively little cost.

Another important advantage to monitoring the environment and developing a working relationship with the library's facilities personnel is that the head librarian and library board will have data needed to develop a plan to improve the environmental controls in the library. Without such data, it will be difficult to find support for raising the funds necessary to make large improvements in the library's environmental conditions.

New Building Projects

When beginning a significant remodeling project or building a new library building, it is important to ensure that the new space has the best environmental controls possible. When coping with an older building that may or may not have been designed to be a library, one has to do the best one can to optimize the environment. However, when building a new facility, or significantly remodeling an existing structure, it is relatively inexpensive to significantly improve environmental conditions. Begin working with the architects and engineers early in the planning process, to ensure they are giving proper consideration to the HVAC system and other factors affecting the environmental conditions of the library. HVAC systems, insulation, and window designs all greatly affect the environmental conditions. Decisions about these systems are generally made very early in the planning process. In short, get involved early, and stay involved!

Fortunately, the environmental needs of library collections dovetail nicely into other concerns architects have when considering HVAC systems. Energy efficiency is extremely important in modern buildings. Efforts to reduce energy costs are generally beneficial to the preservation concerns for library collections. However, that does not mean you can let your guard down. Talk to the architect and engineers in charge of the project, and if they do not have the experience or expertise needed to give the library the environmental controls it needs, then hire a consultant to work with the planners. There are many consultants throughout the country who can help to ensure that the right kinds of considerations are made for the environmental needs of the collections. In addition, secure a copy of the National Information Standards Organization (NISO) technical report, *Environmental Guidelines for the Storage of Paper Records*, by William K. Wilson, TR01-1995. This document will be of great use to you in explaining your concerns to the architects and engineers and will help guide them in making their decisions.

Conclusion

Environment is important because it is the one area of preservation that can affect all the materials stored in the library. If the environmental conditions are good, the result is that proactive measures are being made twenty-four hours a day, 7 days a week, 365 days a year, to preserve the library's entire collections. Making major improvements to the environmental conditions of a library can often be prohibitively expensive. However, in nearly every library there are several small, inexpensive steps that can be taken to improve the environmental conditions.

Being aware of the environmental needs of your library's collections and the existing conditions will enable you to find ways to optimize conditions. Consistent monitoring will help you identify ways to better control the temperature and relative humidity in the library. Identifying major problems with the building's infrastructure will enable the library to make long-term planning efforts to continually improve the library environment, and will allow you to raise these concerns in a meaningful way to the college, library board, or city officials.

The remaining chapters in the book will provide meaningful, practical suggestions for preserving your collections, but no effort will have as advantageous and long-lasting benefit toward preserving your collections as improving your environmental conditions.

Note

1. James M. Reilly, Douglas W. Nishimura, and Edward Zinn, *New Tools for Preservation* (Washington, DC: Commission on Preservation and Access, 1995), 7.

Chapter 3

Use Patterns

Before an effective strategy can be developed for preserving a library's collection it is important to determine what materials get used, how they are used, and who are the primary users. These questions can be answered through carefully conducted statistical surveys. There are excellent publications that explain how to conduct various surveys to obtain specific kinds of information—whether it is usage patterns, condition of the collections, or patron information needs.[1] There are also many service bureaus and consultants throughout the country who will contract to conduct library surveys.

Surveys are important, but librarians must also apply their rich experience to determine the preservation needs of their collections. Careful, long-term, documented observation about collection use, damage to materials, and types of materials in the collections can be invaluable in determining the preservation needs of a library. Often, when teaching preservation courses in libraries, I will take the participants out into the stacks and have them tell me about what they see. Take a careful walk through your library and see what materials get used, and how these materials hold up to the use—and abuse—of library patrons. Some questions to ask are as follows:

- Does your library prebind books or provide other shelf-preparation treatments such as stiffening paperbacks or reinforcing dust jackets? If so, how do these items hold up to use?
- Do prebound or stiffened covers hold up better than nontreated books?
- Can you identify a pattern in how or where treated materials fail? If so, what can be done to address this inherent weakness?
- Are prebinding or other shelf-preparation efforts cost effective? Does your library regularly have to rebind materials again anyway? Do the majority of nonpretreated items last throughout their useful live without strengthening?

The answers to these questions will be different for each library, but there are some general guidelines in this chapter that will help libraries think about their collections in new ways.

Even if a condition survey was done in the past, if it is more than about five years old the results may no longer be valid because of the dramatic changes in use patterns brought about by the increase of electronic publications.

Gathering Data

There are many ways to gather statistically valid information that will help you in identifying the preservation needs of your collections. Some involve selecting random samples of books and examining those books in a consistent way. Collection surveys can provide a wealth of information in a relatively short amount of time. However, many libraries routinely collect lots of information that can be useful in assessing the preservation needs of their collections. For example, circulation records can be loaded into a database program that can identify what kinds of books circulate; how many times, on average, materials are checked out; what age groups borrow the most materials, and so forth.

Another simple way of identifying how materials get used and how they fail is to gather data on items that have been set aside for repair, rebinding, replacement, or withdrawal. Over a period of time extending several months, record the following information about each damaged book that is pulled from circulation:

- What kind of book is it (e.g., popular novel, children's book, or "how to" book)?
- What kind of binding does the book have (e.g., paperback, hardbound, or prebound)?
- How many times did the item circulate?
- What kind of damage caused the book to be pulled from circulation?

Using this data a library can identify what kinds of books are failing and why. Such information is invaluable for helping the library make informed purchasing decisions about what kind of materials to buy for the library, what kind of bindings these materials should have, and what kind of preshelving treatments are most effective. Such information can also be useful for determining which in-house repair techniques are effective and which are not.

In addition to collecting information about materials pulled from circulation because of damage, libraries can survey their stacks to learn a great deal about the physical condition of the materials in their collections. A randomly selected sample of only a few hundred books can provide a wealth of general information about the collection, provided the survey is well prepared and conducted in a statistically valid manner.

Using a Database

In the long run it will be most effective if this data is recorded directly into a computer database program. All database programs enable you to establish forms with pull-down menus or other such lists that will make data entry easier and more consistent. For the purpose of analysis, it is very important that data be recorded in a uniform and consistent way throughout the data-gathering process; otherwise the analysis will have little meaning. Initial time invested in careful planning and developing the database tables and forms is extremely important. Taking the time to develop a thoughtful and useful survey tool will result in a tool that provides useful information and that can be used and reused throughout the years.

Using database software can be a bit confusing at first. Setting up tables and survey forms involves thinking about things in new ways. It is not unlike learning mathematics or a new language. At first it is hard and confusing, but then it starts to make sense and you begin to understand how database programs work and how they organize and analyze data. Often people who are very comfortable working with computers and use them regularly will still be frustrated when first using database software. Some computer experience does translate over, but much does not. Being aware of these frustrations before you begin will help you stick to the project through the tough beginning stages. The first survey project is always the hardest because there are so many new things to learn and bugs to work out of the system, but you will find that each project gets easier and faster. In addition, the experience gained by library staff in gathering preservation-related information will carry over into other areas of the library. The staff will discover new ways of gathering information and assessing services that will result in improved services to the community.

There are lots of free or low-cost survey applications programs that are very flexible and can be used to create assessment tools for your needs. Most of these are designed to send out email surveys, but you can use them to collect information yourself about your collections. These packages are also helpful in providing some guidelines on the statistical analysis of the data.

Sample Survey

Each library will want to create its own survey instrument to meet the specific needs of its collection. As will be discussed further in later chapters, each library has strengths and weaknesses that will impact its preservation program.

For example, some fortunate libraries have skilled staff to provide basic book repair. Other libraries find themselves serviced by a good library binder that can meet most of their binding and repair needs. If a library has an active and developed book-repair program, the survey will need to be structured in a way that will gather specific information that will help the library plan for how many items need in-house repair. This information will help the library plan staff time, supply expenses, and possible ways to improve the in-house treatments if the survey reveals inherent weaknesses in any of the treatments being performed.

Following is a sample survey that a small academic or public library might wish to use. Using this survey as an example, we will walk through the process of designing a survey including deciding on the questions to ask, designing a database table, and creating a survey form.

The first thing to decide is what information your library wants to gather. The survey below works well for many libraries, but if your library has a local history collection or a genealogical section, you would want to modify the imprint dates and/or the type of volume in order to gather information that will be more useful to your preservation planning efforts. This decision will affect how you conduct the survey. For example, more general information can be gathered using a smaller sample. To gather detailed information about the collection it will require a larger random sample to be statistically valid.

The example survey in table 3.1 was created to provide a library with some general information about the condition of its collections and would require a library to sample about 250 books to get a statistically valid sample. First a library must develop a list of survey questions. These questions are based on what information you want to gather about your collections. Next, you need to define terms so that all the people involved in the survey answer questions consistently throughout the process. It is wise to also create a glossary of terms and detailed written instructions explaining the parts of the survey that might be confusing. In the following example I have placed some brief notes of explanation or clarification in a second column. Many of the terms used in this survey are explained further in the glossary at the back of this book.

After the survey questions are prepared and carefully reviewed to ensure they provide your library with the needed information, a database can be created to store the survey data. It is important to carefully construct your table from the beginning because after it is full of data it is difficult to change. Generally speaking, it is best to assign a field in your table for each question asked. Because each survey program is a little different, I will not show an example of a table, but I thought it would be helpful to demonstrate how the above survey questions can be turned into an easy-to-use computer form.

Table 3.1. Survey questions and explanatory text

Type of volume (choose most accurate description): Monograph Serial Reference work Children's book Popular fiction "How to" book Popular magazine	This question helps you identify what kinds of materials are getting used and how these different types hold up to use. This information, combined with answers from other questions, will be helpful when making future decisions about buying paperbacks, publisher hardbound volumes, or library-bound editions. It will also help you decide on how effective your preshelving preservation efforts have been.
Imprint date: 2010– 2000–2009 1990–1999 1980–1989 1970–1979 1960–1969 1940–1959 pre-1940	The dates selected for this section are based on a library without any special collections. For libraries with older collections more date choices should be added because older items present many preservation challenges not faced by newer materials.
Type of binding: Publisher binding Publisher paper binding Pamphlet Library cloth binding Library laminated graphic-cover binding	Identifying the kind of binding will be useful for learning the various strengths and weaknesses of these binding types.
Condition of text block (mark all that apply): In good condition In fair condition Broken text block Loose pages Damaged pages Missing pages	It is important to identify whether a library's books are failing due to the binding or the text block. If the bindings fail then you can take preventive steps to fight against this either by purchasing books with stronger bindings or through preshelving treatments to strengthen the binding. If a text block fails, that is a different issue because there are fewer options to fight against this weakness.

(continued)

Table 3.1. *(continued)*

Condition of binding (mark all that apply): In good condition In fair condition Damaged spine Loose joints Damaged inner joints Damaged paper cover	In both questions about the condition of the binding and the text block, the first two choices are "in good condition" and "in fair condition." The first choice is self-explanatory—it simply means there is nothing wrong with the item. In fair condition means the item might be slightly damaged or worn a little but that it has not failed to the point necessary to treat it in some way.
Last circulation: Never circulated Previous year Previous five years Previous ten years Restricted use collection	It is useful to know if a volume has ever circulated and the last date it circulated. This information can be useful in weeding projects, but it also helps you decide what kind of preservation treatment to give an item. A volume that has not circulated for a long time or circulates rarely does not warrant the same kind of treatment as a book that circulates regularly. This data can be obtained from the circulation system if the barcode is scanned (see below).
Number of circulations in last five years: 0 1-5 6-10 11-20 20-40 40-60 More than 60	This data, combined with the last question, lets you know the complete circulation history of a volume. Many books circulate a great deal while they are new, but not as much after a few years. This information can be useful in both planning how to treat damaged items and planning for the number of copies of a title to keep in the library. The data comes from the same source, but it is broken down in two questions to emphasize how the data is analyzed in two different ways.
Previous preservation treatments (mark all that apply): Mended pages	It is important to identify what preservation treatments have been done in the past and how well they hold up over time. This information is very

Library binding In-house cover repair Paperback cover stiffener Dust-jacket cover	important, for example, in determining if money spent on preshelving treatments is cost effective. The data from this question, combined with the data from questions about damage to the volume, allows the library to determine the effectiveness of its preservation treatments.
Other information:	It is a good idea to put a free-text field in the survey tool that will allow you to type in any additional information or notes you might wish to include about the item such as identifying items needing immediate attention. Most of the time this field will be left blank, but you will be glad it is there when you need it.
Barcode number:	Scanning the barcode will allow you to pull circulation data and bibliographical information about the volume.

The sample survey form in figure 3.1, which was created on Microsoft Access, provides a good picture of what is possible. The form is created with pull down menus for each question with each pull down list providing the scripted answers listed above. All but two fields on the form require an answer or it will not let you proceed. This ensures that the form is filled out completely for each item in the survey. The fields "Other Information" and "Call Number" are optional and can be left blank. Filling out the form is as easy as clicking on the menu with your mouse and selecting the desired answer.

Another nice feature you can add to your survey form is to have small help messages appear for each question. You can set up the database so that for each question a short explanation appears in the bottom, left-hand corner of the screen on the status bar. On the highlighted question in figure 3.1, you can see that the question, "When was this volume published?" appears in the bottom of the screen.

After the data is collected, you will learn just how powerful database software can be in helping you to analyze your collections. Not only will you be able to successfully predict such things as what percentage of the collection has received previous preservation treatment, or what percentage needs repair,

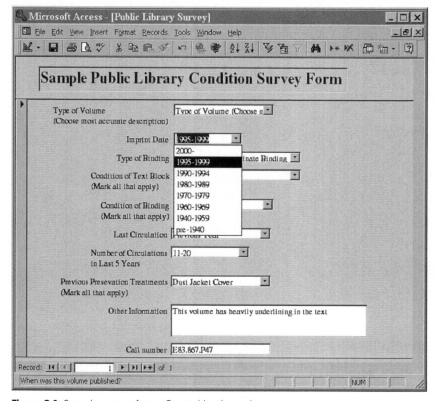

Figure 3.1 Sample survey form. *Created by the author.*

but also you will be able to combine data from questions to learn, for example, what percentage of paperback volumes have cover stiffeners placed on them and how well they have held up over time. You will be able to learn if dust-jacket covers protect the books or if they actually cause the joint area to fail more quickly.

Conducting the Survey

Developing an appropriate survey instrument that gathers the information needed by your library is a very important part of any collection condition survey. The other part that is equally important is the statistical part of the project. If the survey is not conducted properly, the resulting information will not accurately reflect conditions in the collection.

Statistics are challenging. The literature is full of familiar terms such as sample, distribution, mean, mode, and median that are used in unfamiliar ways. There are many well-written articles and books that can help you in structuring your survey and evaluating your data in a statically valid way. However, it is generally a good idea to get the advice of an expert for the statistical part of the survey. Put together your survey, decide what information you want, and then find an expert who is willing to review your work and give you advice. Every college and university will have statistical experts who can assist you. Also, most social scientists have extensive training in statistics to do their work; therefore, it should be relatively easy to find an expert who will volunteer his or her services or offer assistance at a reduced price.

There are some general rules that can help you in the initial preparation of your survey. First, the size of your survey sample will be determined by the level of detail of the information you are gathering. For example, political polls are valid to within a few percent points with sample sizes in the hundreds. It does not matter that there are over three hundred million people in the country, a sample of a few hundred people will give the same results as a survey of thousands. That is the beauty of statistics. This is possible because of the homogeneous nature of the population and the relatively few choices in how the questions can be answered. By contrast, a survey to find out how people around the world feel about some United Nations policy would require a larger sample because the world population is not as homogenous as the population of an individual nation. Furthermore, if the survey were intended to identify how various nations felt about the UN policy, it would take a much larger sample in order to gather enough data about each individual nation.

In most small academic and public libraries, a sample of about 250 books will be sufficient to provide statistically valid information using a survey similar in complexity to the sample provided above. It will even allow for some cross-analysis such as knowing if paperback novels circulate more than hardbound novels.

After it is determined how many items must be sampled to provide you with the information you need, then you can decide how best to collect your sample. The key point is to ensure the sample is randomly selected. This means that each item in the collection has an equal chance of being selected for the survey. There are various strategies that can be employed when selecting a sample. One way is to pull a random sample of titles from your library's online catalog using a database program. It is relatively easy to design a query that will select a random sample from the online catalog and pull the title, author, call number, and other information from the catalog into the database. Then you simply survey the selected titles. One advantage to this method is it gives you bibliographical information on every title that is surveyed. Such data can be useful in conducting longitudinal studies (the process of collecting data on the same population over a long period of time) on your collection. By surveying the same titles five or ten years later you can compare the two results and learn things about your collection you could not learn any other way.

Another easy way of selecting a random sample of your collections is to use a rule or set procedure for selecting items. A good way of selecting a sample is to determine how many items you need, determine how many shelves there are in the library, and then divide the number of samples needed into the number of shelves. For example, say you needed three hundred items for your sample and your library has 1,234 shelves. To get a valid random sample you will need to select a book from every fourth shelf. This will result in getting more than three hundred volumes but not too many more. Remember, when selecting a survey sample the important number is always given as a minimum, not as an exact number. If you need to survey 300 books, 325 will not make your survey more valid, but fewer than 300 will statistically weaken your results.

Next, devise a rule for selecting an item from the appropriate shelf. Some people measure from the left or right side and pick the item that is twelve or fifteen inches from the edge. This works, but I prefer to count books. Generally, I will select the fourth or fifth book from the left edge of the appropriate shelf. I use a number like four or five because too high a number like ten or twelve will require a great deal more time for the surveyors because they will have to count two or three times as many books on each shelf before identifying the needed volume. I also always count from the left-hand side of the shelf because items are shelved from left to right leaving the empty space on a shelf on the right.

How you decide what book to take is not as important as the rule you follow. You need to clearly identify how you will select the survey items and stick to the rule. Your rules must address what you will do if the selected shelf is empty or if the selected shelf has fewer than the required number of books. For example, my survey rules often instruct the sampler to count empty shelves but that if a shelf selected by the rule is empty to move on to the next available shelf with books. If my sampling technique requires me to take the fourth book and a shelf has only three books on it, my rule states to move to the next shelf and take the first available item.

How you physically decide to conduct the survey is another important decision. Some people find it easiest to pull the survey items from the stacks, place them on a book truck, and take them to an office or work space to conduct the survey. Some people prefer to survey the items in the stacks using a laptop computer, a tablet, or a smartphone application. This works well if you conduct the survey as a two-person team where one can evaluate the item and the other person enters the data.

Organize the survey form in a way that will make surveying easy and efficient. Survey each item the same way, answering each question in turn so you develop a pattern and rhythm. Notice the survey questions in the sample survey. They were organized in a logical way to proceed from the outside of the book to the inside. First you identify the type of book, then the type of binding, and then the imprint date, which for this survey involved getting the date off of the call number label. Next you open the book to learn about the text block and the binding; finally, you end with the circulation information, which for this survey was taken off date-due slips in the back of the book. Technology has developed so that the imprint information and the circulation data can be pulled from the online system after scanning the barcode.

Another advantage to developing a well-documented and proceduralized survey method is it will help in the training process if the library decides to organize a team to conduct the condition survey.

Being consistent in how you conduct the survey will save a great deal of time, but it will also result in better survey results. Consistency will ensure that survey questions will not be skipped—requiring you to go back and complete it when the survey form will not clear. It will also result in survey questions being answered in a more standard, methodical way, which will produce better overall results.

One final point in conducting the survey is to try to make technology work for you. There are many wonderful technological advances taking place with computers, tablets, and smartphones. Equally important are the advances in software applications to help you easily collect and process data. Scanning the barcode will enable you to do longitudinal studies in the future and will provide bibliographic information on the items surveyed. However, an equally important fact to remember is that simpler is better. The more complicated the procedures or system, or the more technology that is involved, the more potential there is for something to go wrong. Too often people start to act like kids in a candy store who want all the information they can gather. Just because you can gather the information does not necessarily mean you should gather it. Stay focused on what you really need out of the survey, and do not allow yourself to get distracted chasing after less relevant data.

Analyzing the Data

After the data is gathered from a survey the important work begins. Through careful analysis a library can gain a wealth of information about its collection. The analysis involves statistical expertise. Inappropriately analyzed data can actually be worse than having no assessment information at all. The classic mistake with statistical analysis is to try to gain more information from the findings than the data can support. After the data is gathered, a statistical expert can readily analyze the data or assist you in analysis to ensure proper results are obtained and that those results are properly interpreted.

For the most part, the information collected in library condition surveys is nominal data, meaning that data has no numeric value. The data is similar to a list of names. This means you can get counts on the data and percentages, but there is little room for comparative analysis. This makes the statistics simple and straightforward to analyze.

After the data is analyzed, and reviewed by an expert for accuracy, the library has powerful information that will help in making preservation and collection-development decisions, which leads us to our next chapter.

Note

1. See, for example, Brian J. Baird, *Library Collection Assessment through Statistical Sampling* (Lanham, MD: Scarecrow, 2004); Audrey F. Bancroft et al., "A Forward-Looking Library Use Survey: WSU Libraries in the 21st Century," *Journal of Academic Librarianship* 27, no. 3 (1998): 216–24; Thompson Randolph Cummins, "Survey Research: A Library Management Tool," *Public Libraries* 27 (Winter 1988): 178–81; and Anne Reynolds, Nancy Carlson Schrock, and Joanna Margaret, "Preservation: The Public Library Response; A Preservation Survey of the Public Library in Wellesley," *Library Journal* 114 (February 15, 1989): 128–32.

Chapter 4

Collection Development

It is ineffective to try to determine the preservation needs of a library's collections outside of the context of its collection-development plan. Conducting preservation efforts outside of the collection-development context will result in ineffectively used resources and frustration. This is because there are so many preservation-related decisions made as part of the collection-development process. A condition survey is conducted to determine the preservation needs of a collection, but the findings also have a direct impact on the collection-development plan. For example, the results of a preservation assessment will yield findings on the kinds of physical formats that receive the most use and the subject areas most heavily trafficked. In addition to identifying which collections need preservation care, the survey results can also help guide the collection-development efforts to strengthen the collection. These findings are of particular importance in the electronic information age where titles are available in multiple formats. Knowing what formats are most being used is important information for both the preservation plan and the collection-development policy.

Small academic and public libraries face many unique and challenging collection-development issues. In addition to deciding what titles and subject areas to buy for the collection, the decision must also be made about how many copies to purchase. There are also many preshelving options available for library materials. Therefore it is very important to determine which choices are cost effective for your library and which ones are not. Take, for example, a new novel that has been published from a very popular writer. You know your library needs to purchase this title, but how many copies are needed and in what format? You buy access to the e-book edition, but how many paper copies do you buy? There are several options available. You can buy several copies of the hardbound book, place them on the shelves knowing they will be destroyed in a few months by constant, heavy use, and then they can be replaced by paperback copies when they become available. Another option is to never purchase the paperback version but instead have the hardbound editions commercially bound when they begin to break down. Depending on your binding contract this may be more cost effective than purchasing new paperback editions. Then there are decisions to make about what—if any—preshelving treatments should be given to the items. Are dust-jacket covers placed on the books? Are some volumes sent to be library bound immediately before they are ever shelved? These are hard questions, and the answers are probably a little different for every library depending on the needs of the collection and the resources available. However, the results of the condition survey can help answer these questions.

Book-Selection Process

There are many preservation-related questions to ask during the book-selection process. For example, there are many titles that can be purchased simultaneously as e-books and publisher hardcover bindings, publisher paperback bindings, or in specially prepared bindings designed to hold up to library use. When the option is available, is it better to buy a few hardcover copies of a title, or is it better to buy several paperback copies that are less expensive? Multiple paperback copies will result in more access to a title, but they do not last as long as hardcover books, and hardcover bindings do not last as long as library bindings. Which choice is best depends on the title itself. If a title does not circulate very often, dollars spent on sturdier bindings are not well used. For this reason it is important for a library to know its collection's usage patterns.

Book-selection practices must also take the library's shelf-preparation operations into consideration when determining what format of a book to buy. Properly used shelf-preparation techniques can significantly extend the life of a book—no one will argue otherwise. The question is not so much about effectiveness as about efficiency. Is it cost effective to spend the extra money to provide support for materials before they go to the stacks? Could these dollars be spent more effectively in another way? Again, these are tough questions, but the answers are important. Book-selection practices that take into account the cost-effectiveness of various preservation decisions will eventually translate into significant savings for the library, meaning better services and more materials for the patrons.

One area of collection development that is highly library specific, and needs more general research, is the use of children's books. There are many companies that provide various types of prebound children's books. It needs to be determined what products survive best, how children's books fail, and what can be done to prevent this. One real problem with children's books is that most vendors work to strengthen the covers when it is the pages in the volume that most often fail. Children's books are often printed on thick, stiff, short-fibered paper that tears with surprising ease. Furthermore, the books are often large—especially in proportion to a child. The result is that the child generally turns the pages of a book from the bottom of the page near the inner margin. The result is that little fingers often tear through the paper near the gutter. A quick survey of children's books in any public library will readily demonstrate this problem. Besides training users about how to care for books, there is little that can be done. Therefore, the real question is, do the pages in children's books survive long enough to justify the cost of a strengthened cover? The answer to this question can hugely impact the purchasing decisions and strategies of a library, and this is just one of many such policy decisions that will have a long-term impact on the library's collection-development policy.

Shelf-Preparation Strategies

Shelf-preparation activities are the most cost-effective preservation efforts small academic and public libraries can make for individual titles. The following techniques each greatly extend the life of books at a minimum of staff effort and cost. Furthermore, these activities can all be easily performed by volunteers or vended to a technical-processing service bureau. The question is when to apply them and when not to apply them. In some cases, it is simply easier to have these treatments applied universally to all new titles by a service bureau or vendor. If they are performed in-house, it might be wise to pick and choose a little more carefully.

There are many companies and vendors who provide various kinds of dust-jacket covers, paperback stiffeners, and other shelf-preparation materials. These products are all designed a little different from one another. Most of the companies provide fairly good instructions on how to use their products; therefore, this manual does not provide step-by-step instructions on how to use these products. Rather, the following section provides some general guidelines for libraries to consider when using these products.

Book Training

Every child used to be taught in elementary school how to train a book, but now it seems to be a lost art. Training a book is a way of evenly breaking in the spine of a volume. This ensures that the volume opens well and greatly reduces the chance of the spine cracking.

Training is performed by placing a book on a table holding the text block vertically and with the front and back covers laying on the table at ninety-degree angles from the text block (see figure 4.1). Beginning at the front of the book, peel the first ten to twenty pages of the book away from the text block toward

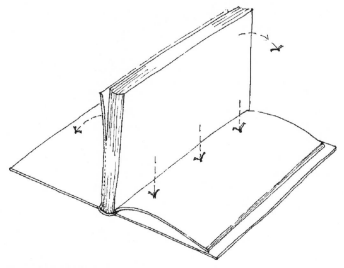

Figure 4.1 Book training

the front cover, applying gentle pressure along the inner margin or gutter. Next, do the same thing with the last ten to twenty pages of the book. Continue this process, ten to twenty pages at a time, working toward the center of the book from both the front and back of the book, applying even, gentle pressure on the inner margin of the volume.

Book training is always important, but it is especially vital on adhesive bound volumes that are much more likely to crack if not properly trained. Proof of the importance of this procedure can be seen in any library's paperback novel collection. Some books are used gently the first several times they are read and, as a result, become well trained. These volumes very rarely develop split spines. In fact, the stress is so evenly distributed across the spine that they eventually develop a concave shape. By contrast, notice paperbacks that do not have this curved shape to their spines and you will be able to find one or more spots where the spine is broken. Once the adhesive is broken on a book it will last only a few circulations at most before pages start to fall out.

Book training is perfect work for volunteers. It is quick and easy to train a person to do this properly and can be done while sitting at a table or desk. Book training is not a service that most service bureaus offer. However, it is probably a service they would be willing to offer if enough libraries were interested. It does not take a great deal of time and can be easily done either by the staff at the library or by a vendor when the item is checked to see that it matches the order and is properly printed and bound.

This effort alone will probably do more to extend the life of a book and reduce repair and rebinding costs than any other preventative treatment. There are things that can be done to strengthen covers on paperbacks and hardbound items, but if a book is not trained the text block can still break quickly regardless of what is done to strengthen the cover.

Dust-Jacket Protectors

Other than book training, dust-jacket protectors are one of the best uses of preservation resources. Dust-jacket protectors provide several important functions. They protect the dust jackets, thus making this information available for use by patrons in selecting a title. As a general rule, dust-jacket flaps are the only source of information about the author of the book and are the only place where a summary of the book can be found. Also, people often know what a book looks like and so when they come to the library and browse the shelves they are often looking for design elements of a familiar dust jacket to jump out at them rather than looking at call numbers or reading titles. Furthermore, the foil stamping on the spines of modern books does not last very long. The color soon flakes off after just a few uses. The result is a shelf full of very similar looking books with little or no title information. Patrons like dust jackets and are generally grateful when they are preserved.

Dust-jacket protectors guard the covers of the books from abrasion and damage. Most popular novels are published using paper sides and even paper on the spines. If cloth is used on the spine it is generally very thin and weak. These covers do not hold up well to the daily use and abuse library books suffer. Books that do not have dust-jacket protectors will regularly develop cover damage on the spine because patrons and library staff members often remove volumes from the shelf by pulling on the head cap or hooking their fingers in the hollow of the spine. A plastic dust-jacket protector supports the spine of the cover and prevents damage. The plastic also protects from damage by water or other spilled liquids. It is amazing how many volumes can be found in any library that exhibit stains, cup rings, coffee spills, or other kinds of damage from liquids on their covers.

A word of caution: Only use dust-jacket protectors that do not permanently adhere to either the dust jacket or the book. Over time the protectors wear out and must be replaced. If the protector is glued or heavily taped to either the dust jacket or the book cover, it will make replacing the protector difficult or impossible. Also, make certain that the plastic used in the dust-jacket protector contains no vinyl, which will yellow, shrink, and become brittle. One relatively quick and easy way to attached dust-jacket covers to a book without actually adhering the cover to the binding is to use strips of Mylar film and double-sided tape. Make tabs like the one shown in figure 4.2. This can be done by placing

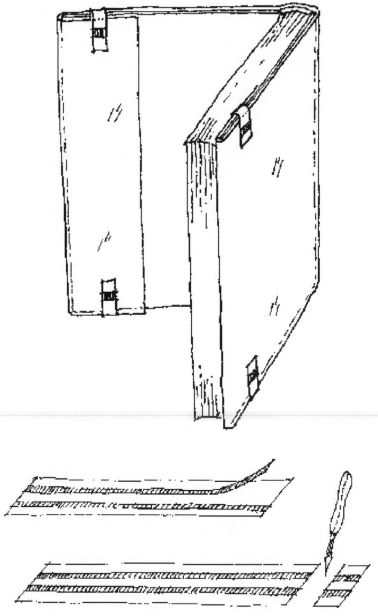

Figure 4.2 Applying dust-jacket protector to not adhere to the book

two parallel lines of double-sided tape on a strip of Mylar that is about two inches wide. Then this long strip of Mylar can be cut in one-inch-wide sections to produce the tabs. To use these tabs, remove the protective film from the tap and adhere the tab to the inside of the dust-jacket protector. The tab is then pulled tight over the edge of the book and adhered to the inside flap of the dust-jacket protector as shown.

Paperback Cover Stiffeners

Several different products exist for stiffening and protecting paperback covers. Some of these products work very well, while others are detrimental to the volume. Choose a material that is very flexible. It does not require a very thick material to effectively stiffen and protect a paperback cover. If too stiff a material is used it will literally tear the paperback cover off of the text block!

Choose a material that contains no vinyl and uses a pure acrylic adhesive. Contact paper is designed for lining kitchen cabinets and drawers and is readily available in the local supermarket or hobby store, but it is *not* a viable material for stiffening your paperbacks. It will yellow, shrink, and eventually peel away from the cover, leaving a sticky mess.

Though often effective, paperback stiffening can be very dangerous. Unlike dust-jacket protectors, this process is not reversible. Furthermore, it involves applying a very sticky adhesive to the volume. The adhesive can ooze, or the stiffening material can separate from the paperback cover—especially if a treated volume gets too near a heat source such as direct sunlight or a heating vent. This can result in a sticky mess that attracts dirt and leaves a sticky residue on everything the book touches.

To reduce the risk both of oozing adhesive and of the stiffener peeling away from the cover, it is best to wrap it around the edge of the cover, adhering it to the inside of the paperback cover at the top, bottom, and front edges (see figure 4.3). This takes a little extra time, but the finished result is much more aesthetically pleasing, will provide better protection, and will last longer.

Some vendors who supply paperback-stiffening materials also instruct libraries to adhere a strip of thin, plastic, tape-like materials in the inner gutters of the book. The tape is intended to secure the cover to the text block. This is not a wise practice. The tape does indeed ensure that the cover remains adhered to the first and last pages of the book, but it also causes stress on the text block, causing the first and last leaf of the book to separate from the rest of the text block. The result is the cover separates from the text block even faster than it would if the self-adhesive plastic was never added to the gutter. In addition, the

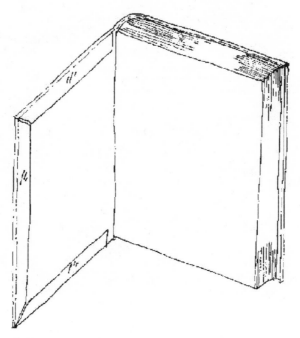

Figure 4.3 Properly applied paperback stiffener

plastic material causes problems for library binders when they have to rebind the book. If the item is sent to the commercial binder, the adhesive used to rebind the book does not stick to the plastic tape, causing a permanent weak spot in the binding. Furthermore, the tape cannot be easily removed from the paper without causing significant damage.

Your library may be performing other kinds of preshelving treatments designed to extend the life of the materials purchased. Use the condition survey to learn if these treatments are producing the desired results and are cost effective. Some things are effective but not cost efficient. There is no question that a properly used paperback stiffener can extend the life of a paperback volume, but there may be times when an item does not need that extra support. For example, there are some kinds of reference materials that are replaced every few years. These items may not get sufficient use to warrant preshelving treatment. Another example is phone books. Many libraries now use electronic phone books, but some places still collect and shelve dozens of phone books for the city or town in which the library resides and for surrounding communities. Local phone books probably need support if they are going to survive for even one year, but outlying community phone books get used only occasionally and may not need any support at all.

Chapter 5

Preservation Resources Available

After the needs of the collection are determined, efforts should be directed toward finding ways to meet those needs. In doing so, it is important to evaluate the preservation resources available to your library. For example, some libraries have staff members who are well trained at performing book-repair techniques. Other libraries have favorable contracts or agreements with their library binder. By clearly understanding the preservation needs of the collections, and the resources available that can be assigned to the problems, a library can develop strategies to optimize its preservation efforts.

Many libraries are not fully aware of the preservation resources available to them in their area simply because they have never looked into it. For example, most libraries do employ the services of a library binder, but many are not fully aware of all the services offered by their binder. Likewise, in more populated areas, there are often bookbinding guilds or clubs that may be of service in providing some book-repair training or expertise. There are also a surprising number of training opportunities available where the library staff can get formal training in specific preservation activities. Often this training is available online. Just as it is wise to assess the collection to determine its preservation needs, it is also important to carefully assess the preservation resources available to your library. Assign a staff member or a task force to assess the preservation resources available on staff, in the community, from local vendors, and from service bureaus. This can be a very educational and interesting assignment—especially if the staff member has an interest in learning more about library preservation.

There are many sources of information available. The American Libraries Association (ALA) is always a good source for all sorts of preservation-related information. The Association for Library Collections and Technical Services (ALCTS), Preservation and Reformatting Section (PARS), of ALA is a particularly good source.

There are some very useful web pages that provide lots of preservation-related information. These sites are good for answering specific questions. Conservation OnLine (often referred to as CoOL) is a very large web page with many links to other websites. It also provides access to the archives of several electronic discussion lists and newsletters. This website is designed primarily for use by professional conservators, so some of the information is very technical. However, there is also a wealth of information that is useful to a library interested in furthering its preservation programs. This site can also help you find out about specific preservation professionals and programs in your area. Conservation OnLine was created by Walter Henry, a conservator at Stanford University, and it represents two decades of his work. It is now maintained by the American Institute for Conservation. The address for this site is http://cool.conservation-us.org.

Another useful website for conservation-related information is the Northeast Document Conservation Center (NEDCC) in Andover, Massachusetts. NEDCC is a large, nonprofit regional conservation center. There are several regional conservation centers around the United States. Each center offers slightly different services, but most provide conservation services and preservation planning and consultation for a fee. NEDCC has some useful preservation manuals and other related information on its website that will be useful to academic and public libraries in their preservation planning efforts. The address for the NEDCC website is http://www.nedcc.org.

For more information about the regional conservation centers, visit their website at http://www.rap-arcc.org. This cooperative website provides general information about the regional conservation centers and directs library professionals on how to find out the specific information they need from the regional conservation center in their area.

Finally, a good source of information about preservation is a nearby large university library. Most large research universities have some kind of preservation activity taking place in their libraries. These efforts are led by either a preservation librarian or a preservation team. These experts can often provide a wealth of information about what preservation resources are available in the area. Some of the information they have will be specific to the needs of a large research library that has a very different approach to preservation than a smaller academic or public library, but most of the information will generally be useful. For example, your research university library colleagues can provide you with information such as where to purchase materials for book repair, how to handle disaster recovery efforts, and what library binding resources are available in your area.

One important resource that an academic or public library should never overlook is the state library. Some state libraries have very good preservation programs, but even if they do not, they generally have useful information and expertise that can help your library in planning its preservation program. State libraries have good experience establishing contracts with vendors or service bureaus to provide libraries with the services they need. This experience and expertise can be used to help public libraries secure better binding contracts or cheaper preservation supplies by arranging for these supplies to be purchased in bulk.

Funding

Funding is often the most difficult challenge to establishing a preservation program. An important part of any preservation assessment is identifying what it will cost to implement the preservation options available to your library and what funds are available. When done properly, the assessment process will identify ways of saving money that can then be used to further the library's preservation efforts. However, these savings alone may not produce sufficient funding to meet all of the library's preservation needs. This leaves two remaining options: (1) a reallocation of existing library funding (which can be painful); or (2) raising outside funding for preservation efforts.

Traditionally, preservation has been an attractive area for fundraising efforts. People like to donate money to a cause that will result in preserving their cultural heritage or making information available to future users. If people feel strongly about libraries, then they will also feel committed to preserving the collections housed in the library.

To be successful in fundraising you need three things. First, seek funding for a specific project. Second, you need an interesting story that explains why the funding is needed and what good will result from the money being raised. Third, you need to have something tangible and long lasting to show for the funding. This is why people will give money to help starving children, or will donate to save a historic building that carries fond memories for them. Library preservation offers all of these things. The idea of contributing money to support a library's efforts to preserve their collections and make them available to future generations is very appealing. But that said, with the advent of the World Wide Web, smartphones, and electronic information, people do not feel as strongly about libraries as they once did. They need to be reminded of why they care.

One successful fundraising effort has been to encourage individuals to pay for the preservation of a book in the collection. This is done by asking for a small fixed amount, usually between twenty-five and fifty dollars per book. The contributor is then given a letter thanking him or her for the contribution and identifying the title that has been preserved. A special bookplate is then placed in the volume identifying the person who contributed the funding to preserve the book. As a general rule, it is best to use such a program only on titles that will be permanently kept in the collection. It can be very disheartening to contributors if they see books with these special bookplates in the annual book sale or if they come to the library years later only to find out that the title they paid to have preserved has been withdrawn from the collection.

Another important source of funding is granting agencies—both private and governmental. There are many local or state foundations that are eager to provide funding for public library preservation efforts. Often foundations require no more than a letter of explanation about what the library needs and how the money will be used. Foundations and governmental grants are often secured to help libraries obtain the services of a consultant to help survey the condition of their collections, develop a preservation plan, or sometimes to purchase book-repair equipment.

The most important thing a library needs when trying to raise money for preservation is a specific plan and evidence that documents the library's need. Again, the condition survey helps greatly in providing this information, but having the raw data alone is not enough. It has to be packaged in an attractive way that makes the information immediately accessible and easily understood by the general public. Furthermore, a library needs to have patience. Sometimes fundraising efforts can proceed rapidly, but very often they are driven by serendipity. Every successful fund-raiser will have countless stories about how he or she happened to be at the right place, at the right time, to secure a gift or a grant. The opportunities are out there, but they only result in funding for your library when the necessary preparation work has been done so you can present a clear story about your project in a way that will interest the contributing organization.

Finally, remember that success breeds success. People and organizations are much more likely to fund a program that has proven itself successful. After a library has had some success raising money for a preservation program, it often gets easier to find additional funding from other sources, because people want to back a winner. Successful fundraising efforts always take advantage of this aspect of human nature. There are plenty of organizations that will fund start-up programs, but even these proposals need to be presented in a way that will assure the contributing agency that you are preparing a project that is sure to be successful.

Chapter 6

Library Binding

Library binding (sometimes call commercial binding) has traditionally been the most cost-effective, and widely used preservation treatment for libraries of all sizes. There were a number of reasons for this fact. Library binding was accessible with numerous binderies throughout the country. Also, library binding was cost effective and could be processed with relative ease. It was a standardized product so even if librarians moved from library to library throughout the country, they could work with a new binder with a relatively short learning curve. But with the increase of electronic information, and fewer printed books and journals, library binding has dramatically decreased throughout the country. Libraries nationwide in the United States used to spend a combined one hundred million dollars a year on binding. Now they spend less than fifteen million dollars a year. In the 1990s there were dozens of library binders throughout the country. In 2017 you can count the number of binderies on one hand.

These realities provide important context into how a library should make the most effective use of this important preservation resource. The biggest change is that a library can no longer simply set up a binding processing program and blindly trust their binder. Library staff members have to be educated on what their binder can offer and when to use these services.

The primary challenges most libraries face for making good use of commercial binding are that most librarians have a limited understanding of what a commercial binder can do for their library. Second, many individual libraries do not have the volume necessary to entice binders to offer them reduced prices or optimal service—especially in the current climate. Third, library binding requires a cash layout. Finally, many libraries resist sending materials for commercial binding because they do not like the utilitarian aesthetics of buckram-covered library bindings. We will address each of these objections in turn.

One of the biggest obstacles to library binding is the required outlay of cash. In-house repairs often cost many times the price of a commercial binding, but because of less tangible overhead expenses these costs are not readily apparent. Though the initial funding allocation is often difficult to obtain, once a staff position is added to a library the expense of that position's salary and benefits is generally calculated as an overhead expense rather than as discretionary money. Thus, it becomes natural to view that staff member's time as free. This often results in many libraries wasting resources on repairing materials in-house where the end result is an item that is far weaker and less usable than a commercially bound volume.

Another common problem is a lack of understanding about what services a library binder offers. It is amazing the number of libraries who have staff members in charge of making binding decisions who have never visited their library binder. The old saying that a picture is worth a thousand words is true for visiting your library binder as well. Visiting the bindery can be *incredibly* educational. The visit will help the staff member learn what treatment options are available, how those treatments are performed, and how volumes flow through the bindery.

The visit allows staff members to meet the bindery's customer service staff in person, and it is amazing how a simple visit to the bindery can dramatically improve customer service relations between a library and its bindery. Part of this results from the psychological reality that human beings have a much harder time being unreasonable or combative with a person they have met face-to-face and know as a human being. The human contact of a visit helps remove the impersonal distance that a phone call or email message enables. Another reason for the improved relations is that seeing the bindery and learning how things work helps the library staff and the bindery staff communicate with each other using the same language. The visit adds technical terms and contextual richness to future conversations that greatly helps reduce misunderstandings.

In addition to greatly improving customer service relations, a visit to your library binder enables you to learn what binding options are offered by your binder and discuss how these options might best be used for your library. Over the years I have witnessed hundreds of people experience their first visit to a library bindery. This experience is universally educational and exciting. People are constantly amazed at the volume of work that is processed by the library bindery and the amount of labor that is involved. They are often initially overwhelmed by the factory environment and the rapidity of the work flow. However, after the visit, when they are given a chance to reflect on what they have seen, and ask detailed questions that the tour of the plant inspired, there are very few people who do not leave the tour impressed by what they have seen. Universally, people leave the tour inspired to make better use of their library binder's services and excited by the new preservation options they have learned about that they did not know existed before the visit.

That said, because there are so few binderies left in the country it is not as easy as it once was to visit a bindery. However, technology has helped in this area as well. Some of the larger binders have educational websites, and there are some virtual tours of binders out there as well. These resources are wonderful, but no video or web page can take the place of a firsthand visit to your library bindery. It is time well spent if the option is available to you.

Generally, I advise people to visit their commercial bindery at least twice. The first time is when a new staff member is assigned the responsibility for the library's binding program. This initial visit will help educate the new staff member in ways that cannot be equaled. The second visit should be made after the staff member has been on the job for several months to a year. The first visit can be overwhelming. It is often a new and very strange environment for the library staff. Also, being new on the job they will often miss important details that they will catch on a second visit. The first visit is important, but in many ways the second visit might be even more important.

Library binderies exist because they can offer their services on a large scale, in an extremely efficient way, and at reasonable prices. It is impossible for a library, regardless of its size, to duplicate in-house the cost efficiency of a commercial bindery. There used to be tight competition between library binders in the United States. This competition was primarily driven by large university and research libraries. These large institutions had their choice between several library binders who were eager to secure their business. This competition was healthy for the library binding industry and ensured bindery customers the best quality products and services at the lowest possible prices. The result was that the profit margins on individual books were extremely low—literally no more than a few cents per volume. Therefore, binderies had to rely on volume to keep their businesses viable. But this has changed in recent years. Fewer binderies means less competition. Less volume of work and monopoly-type situations means libraries are not in the same position they once were to demand high-quality service at low prices. The result is that librarians have to become knowledgeable about binding and vigilant about monitoring the quality of the binding and service they are receiving.

These facts present both potential benefits and hindrances to smaller libraries. Because of the library binder's desire for large contracts, they have often been less interested in servicing smaller libraries. But now binderies are hungry for any business they can get, so library binding is still available to any library in the United States even though there are fewer binderies. A library may have to ship their volumes to a bindery in a different state (or even a different time zone), but the services are available to all—for now.

Less competition and fewer volumes to bind is a fact of life every small academic and public library needs to understand. These facts manifest themselves in many ways such as slower service, limited binding options, extra charges, or less responsiveness to your questions and concerns. The result can be a hindrance to a library getting the binding services it needs. However, if approached properly, this economic reality can be used to a smaller library's benefit.

Cooperative Binding Contracts

Small academic and public libraries have long known the value of cooperative efforts to fulfill their missions. They develop lending agreements with neighboring communities, and they work through library systems or the state library to coordinate purchasing discounts or technical services, but often they do not use this strategy to secure commercial binding for the library. Many states have statewide binding contracts. Such a contract provides a library with the means to get library binding at a reduced cost. It also enables library staffs to be confident that they will get the quality binding services outlined in the contract.

If your library is not taking advantage of a statewide contract, first check with the state purchasing department to find out if such a contract exists. Sadly, there are many public libraries—especially in remote areas—that are unaware that they are covered by a statewide binding contract. If your library is not covered by such a contract, begin immediately working with the state library or library systems to ensure that a contract is secured. A consultant can be hired to assist in this process, but smaller libraries in a state can also generally rely on the work of the larger university libraries that almost always have binding contracts or detailed binding agreements established with a commercial bindery. Depending on the logistics of the state, the contracted binder may or may not be willing to extend a university contract to include smaller academic or public libraries. However, if they are not willing to extend an existing contract, the state library can use the bid specifications developed by the university libraries as a boilerplate to create their own bid specifications.

The secret to securing a good binding contract is information. When preparing the bid specifications make sure you are familiar with the latest binding standard. The current standard was jointly developed by the Library Binding Institute (LBI) and the National Information Standards Organization (NISO). It was then accepted by the American National Standards Institute (ANSI). Library Binding ANSI/NISO/LBI Z39.78-2000 (R2010) is a performance-based standard that specifies the performance levels library bindings must meet to be in compliance with this standard. It is an excellent standard, and libraries of all size should rely heavily on this document when preparing bid specifications or binding agreements with a commercial binder. No library should ever enter a contract with any binding vendor who is unwilling to ensure their services and products meet the national binding standard.

The standard has not received significant updates since 2000 when it was first written. It was renewed in 2010 and again in 2015 but does not have a guaranteed future. It is incumbent on the library community to make sure this standard is updated and survives—especially when there is less binding competition and libraries are not spending enough money on binding to use their budgets to demand the service they desire.

Next, understand what vendors serve your area. Most large research libraries in the United States used to have two or more library binders to choose from, but this is not true now for many parts of the country. Understand what competition exists, and use that competition to your library's advantage. This means knowing what binders are out there and whether they will bind for your library, what services they offer, and the quality of their services and products. Use this specific information in preparing the bid specifications. It used to be very common to have a bindery close enough that they would pick up your library binding on one of their trucks. This has become much less common. The downside is that you have to often account for shipping costs as part of your library binding budget. The upside is that you are no longer limited to binding with the closest bindery to your library. You can ship your work to any bindery.

When possible, always use a negotiated bid process to secure a library binding contract. There are many variables to consider when negotiating a binding contract that can often complicate the decision-making process. Rarely does the decision involve straight comparison between costs for specific types of binding. One vendor may offer low binding costs on a volume-by-volume basis, but they may make up for those cost savings in the extra charges they pass on to libraries. For example, some binderies charge for extra lettering on the spine, and some have extra charges for various leaf-attachment methods.

Securing a commercial binding contract is an involved process that works best when done through a negotiated bid process. This will help the participating libraries get the best price and best services possible while, at the same time, not restricting the binder into performing services it does not usually perform, or conducting business in a way not standard for the company. Negotiations allow the participating libraries and the vendor to settle on an agreement that will be a win-win situation for all involved.

A very important aspect of securing a good binding contract is to clearly specify what libraries are covered by the contract and the binding needs of each participating library. This information will be very important to the vendors in helping them figure their costs. It will also help in planning the logistics of servicing the contract area. This is where the cooperative aspect of the bid comes into play. As stated earlier, commercial binders like large accounts that require limited special work. Public libraries can achieve this effect by having a large cooperative contract and by agreeing up front, *before* the contract is signed, what they need from their binder. The effect is that a binder is guaranteed a certain volume of work and that all the work can be processed in a standard, agreed-upon manner.

One of the realities of having fewer library binders is that many of them will no longer offer contracts to libraries that have binding budgets below a certain threshold. The loss of competition means binders are regularly raising this threshold to be significantly higher than what many small academic or public libraries spend. This is yet another reason consortial binding agreements are so important for smaller libraries.

An important component to consider in any cooperative binding agreement is to find ways to limit the shipping expenses of getting work to and from the bindery. If you live in an area where a bindery offers truck service, it is frustrating to the binder to get a contract that requires them to travel hundreds or even thousands of miles around the state visiting many small libraries that may or may not have work for them to do. To alleviate this, and to make your consortial contract more appealing to the binder, take as much responsibility as possible of the shipping arrangements. First, there are many shipping firms and options available. Most library systems already have local courier systems in place, or they have contracts with large international firms such as UPS or Federal Express to provide reduced shipping charges for their interlibrary loan operations. Investigate ways of using a courier service to get the binding shipments to the library binder, or to consolidate small binding shipments from several libraries into one larger shipment or into one central location where the bindery can pick up. This can be done in a number of ways. If the binder is local, then a courier service might be able to effectively and cost efficiently handle all book shipments. Or a hybrid approach can be used. A binding cooperative might be able to take advantage of a shipping system already in place for shipping books from the state library or a service bureau to the various public libraries. Often, purchasing and technical processing of books is all conducted at the state library or at centralized library system offices. If this is the case for your area, then the commercial binder could pick up and deliver binding shipments at a few central locations and these locations could use the routing and shipping system already in place to distribute binding orders to and from the various individual libraries.

Finally, make sure you secure a contract that will last for as long of a time as possible. A great deal of time and effort goes into preparing good bid specifications for binding. The negotiation process is equally taxing. Therefore, it only makes sense to ensure you get a good contract and keep it for as long as possible. This is good for everyone involved. It is good for the libraries because it means they can focus their attention to building good working relations with a vendor who will be around for several years. It is good for the binder because it means they can count on the business from the contract for several years. This will make the bindery more willing to focus its time and energies into offering the best services it can.

What to Bind

Establishing a good binding contract and learning the services offered by your binder are important first steps, but then it is up to the library to develop a strategy for how best to take advantage of their binding resources. One thing to keep in mind about commercial bindings is that they very rarely fail. Research has shown that library bound materials hold up to an incredible amount of use and abuse. The covers are nearly indestructible, and the text blocks are constructed to be very flexible and strong. This is important to remember because nearly every library has more materials in need of binding than they can afford to bind. Therefore, it is wise *not* to bind materials that the library does not plan to hold onto for a long time. I am often amazed at the number of library book sales I visit where several copies of library-bound titles are available for purchase. Again, this is why it is so important to tie preservation planning and strategies into the collection-development plans of a library. It is not wise to bind several copies of a popular novel after the title has received most of its use. Certainly it is a good idea to bind the one or two copies the library intends to keep in the collection long term, but do not bind all of them when several of those copies will go to the book sale within a short time.

Many library binding decisions are easy to make. The library's copy of the latest Webster's dictionary is going to get a lot of use, and it is going to be kept in the library for many years. The key to these decisions is not *if* to bind but *when* to bind. Often the decision to bind is put off too long while futile efforts are made to repair the item in-house one or more times. Often these efforts result in a highly damaged volume that will be more difficult for the library binder to rebind effectively. If it is recognized that a volume will be kept in the library for several years, and that it will receive heavy use, get it bound as soon as the original binding starts to fail. The result will be a sturdy, attractive binding that will withstand hundreds or even thousands of uses.

Other decisions are more difficult. These decisions are made harder because there is often more than one effective treatment decision to be made. These decisions often involve economic issues and library procedures. For example, is it more cost effective for your library to discard the damaged item in hand and replace it with a new copy, or a used copy, or is it better to rebind it? Is it better to commercially bind the item or have it repaired in-house? These questions are more completed by how inexpensive and readily available used books have become, and by how effective interlibrary loan has become. Add to that the option of e-publications. Experience and practice will help make these decisions easier, but the dilemmas will never completely disappear. Two things to remember are the processing costs involved with replacing a book with a new copy—even if the used book is just a few dollars. Also, a used book will often be only a few circulations away from being as damaged as the book it is replacing. Binding is rarely a bad decision. Binding a book results in a ten- to fifteen-dollar bill to produce a binding that will almost certainly last for as long as the library wishes to keep the book on the shelf. Given that fact, I advise libraries that when in doubt about whether to bind or not bind, binding is generally the safest answer.

Binding Options and Decisions

After the decision to bind has been made, the next step is to decide what kind of a binding to get. There are many options available. Most of the binding options described below are offered by nearly every library binder, but you will need to check with your binder to find out what options they have available and what terminology they use to describe the various binding types they offer. Some binders develop clever, even trademarked, names to describe their binding styles.

Text Block

The first decision that must be made is whether or not the paper in the volume is strong enough to withstand rebinding. Currently, there is not a way to strengthen brittle, weak paper, and no covering material, regardless of how strong, will protect a book from damage when the paper is so brittle that it will crack out of the text block. Brittle paper can be easily identified by the double-fold test.

The double-fold test involves folding a corner of a page over on top of itself as if you were dog-earing the page (see figure 6.1). Crease the fold and then fold the paper in the opposite direction on the same fold line. This constitutes one

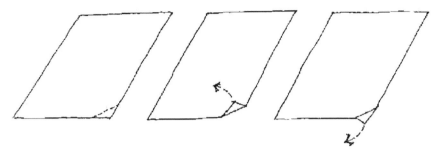

Figure 6.1 How to perform a double-fold brittle paper test

double-fold. Do this twice. If, at any time during this process the corner breaks off, the paper is brittle. Generally speaking, this test only needs to be performed on materials printed earlier than 1960.

In addition to the double-fold test, there are some visual indicators that can help you identify potentially brittle paper. Generally, the acid-degradation process that causes the paper to weaken and become brittle will also darken the paper from yellow to tan and to brown. This is not always true. Some papers will turn brittle while remaining very white in color. Others will darken and still be flexible, but generally, if a paper has darkened it should be tested for brittleness.

As a general rule, I advise libraries not to bind any paper that cannot survive at least one double-fold without breaking. Brittle paper is weak and cannot withstand a great deal of abuse, but often, if a weakened paper can be bound, it will survive many years of additional use—even as it becomes more brittle. This is because a library binding is so flexible that it greatly minimizes the stress placed on the weakened paper.

After it has been determined that the paper in a volume is strong enough to be bound, then you must decide what kind of "leaf attachment" you want. Leaf attachment refers to the method of holding the pages of the text block together prior to case binding it. There are five basic leaf-attachment methods used in library binding. These are briefly explained below. All of these methods, except for polyurethane reactive (PUR) binding, are specifically discussed in the library binding standard.

Double-Fan Adhesive

This method involves chopping or grinding the spine off of the bound item producing loose sheets. The loose pages are then glued together using a double-fan method. The double-fanning process ensures that adhesive is placed

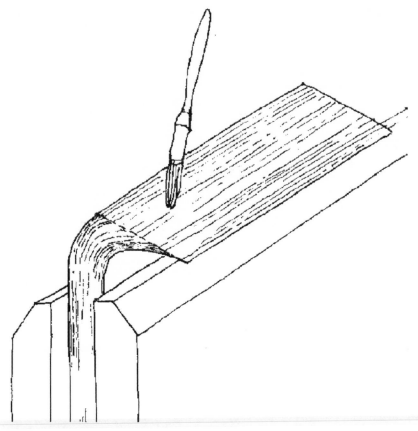

Figure 6.2 Double-fan adhesive binding method

not only on the edge of each loose sheet but also a little onto the surface of each page (see figure 6.2).

This method ensures that a much larger surface area of each sheet is adhered to the adjoining sheet. It is kind of like tipping all of the pages together. The result is a much stronger binding. In recent years there have been great improvements in this binding process, and it has become the default leaf-attachment method for most library bindings. This, in large part, is because so many books and journals are originally bound as adhesive bindings, leaving the binder few other options than to reglue the pages using a stronger process than perfect binding.

Two important advances include notching the spine edge of the loose sheets to create even more surface area for the adhesive to adhere to the pages (see

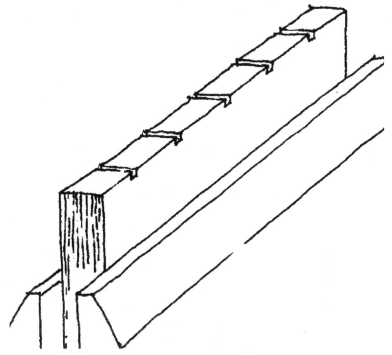

Figure 6.3 Notched pages prior to adhesive binding

figure 6.3). The other is the remarkable advances in adhesives used in library binding. Commercial binders use a polyvinyl acetate (PVA) adhesive. PVA dries clear, strongly bonds to the paper, and remains very flexible when dry. Over the past several years, special glue formulas have been developed for each step in the binding process including double-fan adhesive binding. These new glues are stronger and more flexible than ever before. With the advancements in double-fan adhesive binding, this leaf-attachment method is a very good option to choose under nearly any condition. The one type of paper that still presents some challenges for double-fan adhesive binding is heavily coated, glossy paper as is found in some art and medical-type journals, or in art books or other books with many photographic illustrations such as coffee-table books. PVA adhesive does not bond as well to this glossy paper. These volumes are excellent candidates for saving the original sewing when possible, or for PUR adhesive binding. See below for more details about each of these binding methods.

Oversewing

This used to be the standard leaf-attachment method used in library binding. As with double-fan adhesive binding, oversewing begins with removing the spine of the text block. However, instead of then gluing the pages together, they are sewn together using a large sewing machine. Oversewing works by side sewing the pages together at about a thirty-degree angle. A small stack of the loose leaves (about one-sixteenth-inch [2 mm] thick) is inserted into the oversewing machine, and several needles stab through the pages, leaving behind thread.

Another small stack of loose leaves is placed on top of the sewn ones, and the needles sew through those pages linking the first stack to the second (see figure 6.4). This process continues until the entire book is sewn together. Oversewing produces a very strong leaf attachment, and before the days of effective adhesive binding there was no other option for sewing loose pages together. However, this leaf-attachment method has its drawbacks as well. Because the pages are sewn together from the side, the bound text block is stiff and does not open very well. This leaf-attachment method can produce a book that is difficult to read and nearly impossible to photocopy from if the text block does not have a large inner margin. Oversewing requires about a three-eighth's inch of margin to avoid hitting text with the sewing. So it should only be chosen as an option if there is a large inner margin. Because of the limited openability, this leaf-attachment method should never be used with brittle or weak paper. Another problem with this method is that most books and periodicals are being printed with ever-decreasing inner margins. However, the advantages to oversewing are that it is a strong leaf attachment that very rarely fails, and it works very well on glossy and heavy papers that cannot be easily double-fan adhesive bound. Because of the liabilities of this leaf-attachment method, and because oversewing is a rather time-consuming process, binders will not generally choose to use this leaf-attachment method. Therefore, if you know you

Figure 6.4 How oversewing works

want this leaf-attachment method you will usually need to specify it, and you might be charged extra. Finally, the oversewing machines are no longer being made, and parts are expensive and sometimes difficult to obtain. As a result, this option may not be offered by some binders in the future.

Sew through Fold

This leaf-attachment method primarily refers to sewing periodical binding. This method employs a large sewing machine that sews the issues of a bound periodical together through the fold of each individual magazine issue (see figure 6.5). This method only works when the individual periodical issues are saddle-sewn as are many popular magazines such as *Time*, *Sports Illustrated*, and *People*. This is a very good leaf-attachment method when binding materials that can accommodate it.

It is wise to have your binding contract clearly specify that this is the preferred binding method of choice for your library when possible. The advantages are that the bound volume opens flat, the volume is held together by strong string rather than glue, and no inner margin is lost. That all said, this option is only possible when all (or most) of the issues of a journal are saddle-sewn. Fewer and fewer periodicals are printed in this format, and many journals, such as *American Libraries*, for example, will issue one or two adhesive bound issues a year along with their standard saddle-sewn issues, thus making it difficult or impossible do sew the entire volume when binding.

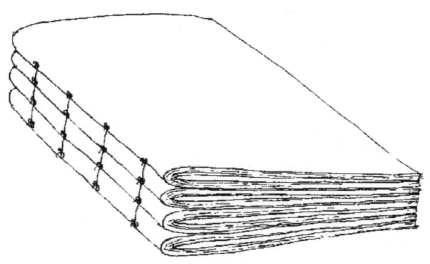

Figure 6.5 Journal volumes that have been sewn through the fold

Save Original Sewing

This method applies to publisher-bound books with sewn text blocks. It involves removing old adhesive and linings from the spine of the text block, attaching new endsheets, and then producing a new case for the book. The advantage to this leaf-attachment method is that it preserves the original sewing and flexibility of the text block. It also prevents any loss of inner margin. This technique is particularly useful for art books or coffee-table books with glossy paper and images that run through the gutter. This method can only be used when the text block is in good condition. It cannot be used if the text block is split or if the sewing is broken. For this reason, if you desire to use this leaf-attachment method, it is wise to send volumes to the binder before they become too damaged to allow the original sewing to be saved. This method may cost a little extra, but it is an excellent option to have when used appropriately. Many libraries will specify this as their preferred leaf-attachment method, meaning the binder will always try to save original sewing whenever possible.

There are a couple of important things to watch for with this leaf-attachment method. Be aware that different binders use different methods for attaching the new endsheets to the text block. Many binders will tip endsheets to the text block. However, the preferred method is to have double-folio endsheets hand sewn onto the text block. Ask your binder about their procedures for attaching endsheets to a text block when the original sewing is being retained. If they tip-in the endsheets, then they should not charge you as much as they would if they sew them on, which is a much more labor-intensive process. Also, the key to producing a good, strong, long-lasting binding is to make sure the original adhesive is thoroughly removed from the spine before the new endsheets are added and a new spine lining is glued to the spine of the text block. This is not always an easy process—especially with some of the more modern, hot-melt adhesives being used in publisher bindings. Make sure you have your binder explain, in detail, how they perform this treatment.

PUR Binding

Polyurethane adhesive has been widely used throughout the medical, packaging, and automotive manufacturing industries for decades. It has been used in the bookbinding industry since the late 1980s as a hot-melt adhesive formula known as polyurethane reactive (PUR). Generally hot-melt glues and perfect-binding adhesive bindings were not strong enough to meet the NISO/Library Binding Service (LBS) binding standard, but PUR is strong enough to meet and exceed the standard. It is a very aggressive adhesive that produces a strong, flexible binding. In 2010 testing was performed that demonstrates that PUR meets the binding standard.[1] Since then several library binders have started using PUR binding as a leaf-attachment method for their binding customers. PUR works very well on all types of paper but is especially suited for glossy paper. It is likely that PUR will become the library-binding industrial standard in the near future just as PVA double-fan binding is now, and that PVA binding will become a secondary option, to be used when appropriate, similar to oversewing or through-fold sewing.

After the text block is bound, there are important decisions that need to be made about the kind of case a volume will receive. There are several covering materials options and some choices to make about rounding and backing. We will look at these options in turn.

Rounding and backing is the process of giving the text block a curved spine and raised shoulders, or its mushroom shape (see figure 6.6).

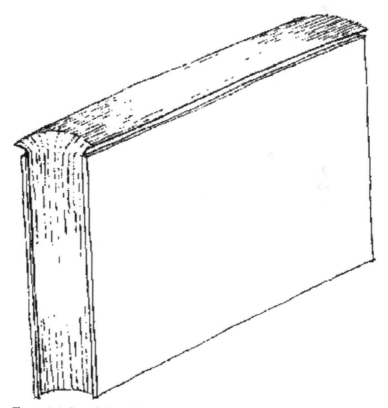

Figure 6.6 Rounded and backed text block

The need for rounding and backing has been hotly debated among library binders. Some binders feel it is important to round and back text blocks; others feel this step is superfluous and adds no structural support. At present there is no conclusive evidence one way or the other on this debate and may become moot in the future since PUR bindings cannot be rounded and backed. But for now, most binders leave the decision to the library. Ask your binder about the options they offer and pricing difference (if any).

My opinion, based on my training as a book conservator and from years of experience in evaluating collections, is that rounding and backing provides some structural support for the text block. It helps the book keep its shape, which translates into fewer loose pages in the text block in the long run. Furthermore, for me, rounding and backing is the safe choice. While the jury may be out on whether rounding and backing helps a bound book last longer, we have generations of experience to show that it certainly does not hurt a text block. Therefore, until there is evidence to show otherwise, I generally choose to have text blocks rounded and backed. Finally, I like rounding and backing because I very much prefer rounded books for aesthetic reasons. I like the traditional look of a curved spine and tighter shoulder joints.

The decision about rounding and backing could affect the binder you choose. Some binders offer little or no rounding backing, while all binders offer non-rounded books—or flat-back bindings. For example, most binders do not offer rounding and backing for their economy-type bindings. Economy bindings offer fewer cloth color selections and employ a weaker cloth or covering material, no rounding and backing, and limited labeling options. Economy bindings are designed for lower-use items and smaller items that do not require as much support. Economy bindings usually cost 20 to 30 percent less than a standard binding with F-grade buckram. If a book receives high use or if it is heavy or thick, it should receive a standard binding.

The type of covering material selected is based on the kind of binding requested. A standard binding employs F-grade buckram. This cloth is a strong poly-cotton, acrylic-coated cloth that is available in fifteen different colors right now. In recent years the number of cloth colors has steadily decreased, and that trend may continue. This cloth is *extremely* strong, wears well, resists moisture and dirt, and stamps beautifully. F-grade buckram is nearly indestructible and is rarely the cause for a commercial binding to fail. Some people do not like the rather utilitarian look of library-bound volumes. Despite the wide range of colors offered in F-grade buckram, they are still all flat, monotone colors with a glossy overcoating. This is a concern for some librarians—especially public libraries. For this reason, commercial binders offer different types of covering materials, but it is important to remember that none of the other options are as strong as F-grade buckram.

Most binders offer three alternate covering options in addition to F-grade buckram. These are B- and C-grade cloths, acrylic coated, paper-based covering material, and laminated graphic covers. Of these options, C-grade cloth is the strongest. C-grade cloths are made of a poly-cotton blend that is quite strong. B-grade cloth is thinner and less strong. These cloths stamp well, as with the F-grade buckram, and have an acrylic coating that resists moisture and soiling as does the buckram, but it is much thinner. B- and C-grade cloths come in a wide variety of colors, but most binders only offer a limited selection. The nice thing about these materials is that they look more like cloth and are not so plastic-like. They are not as monotone and have some texture. This is appealing to some libraries.

The acrylic-coated, paper-based covering material has several different brand names, so ask your binder what they use to ensure you are using the same terminology. This material used to be called "Type II" covering material, and most binders will still know what you are talking about if you ask for that material. Current brand names are Skivertex, Advantage, and Kivar, to name a few. These paper-based materials stamp beautifully and can be textured to look like a cloth. Again, there are many color options available, but most binders only carry a limited selection to choose from. This material is significantly weaker than C-grade cloth. This material wears well, but once it begins to tear it tears relatively easily. The stamped texture on the material is attractive, but the colors are more monotone and flat, similar to the F-grade buckram. Most binders charge less for paper-based material bindings than they do for C-grade cloth covers.

Laminated graphic covers allow a library to retain the graphics and information from the original publisher cover or dust jacket into the new hardbound cover of the rebound item (see figure 6.7). This is done by carefully removing the original paperback cover or the dust jacket, scanning it, printing the scan in color onto a strong paper, and then laminating the paper to provide strength and protection to the cover. When done properly, this covering material produces a very attractive cover. Depending on the lamination process used by your binder the cover material is as strong, or stronger than, some B- and C-grade cloths. The laminate film is resistant to moisture and dirt and can be wiped clean if the book becomes soiled. In order to produce a nice laminated graphic cover, the original paperback cover or dust jacket must be in good condition. The cover cannot be torn, frayed, or bent too much, because all of these imperfections show up in the scan. Some binders offer these laminated graphic covers at no extra charge. Other binders charge extra for them.

Figure 6.7 Examples of graphic laminated covers. *Created by the author.*

One drawback to a laminated cover is that the preservation field is unsure how long these covers will last. All plastics degrade, and when they begin to degrade they degrade very rapidly—especially when subjected to bright sunlight. It may be that these laminated covers will last less than fifty years. That sounds like a long time, but many books are kept in libraries for hundreds of years. Therefore, the long-term effects should be considered when making your covering decision.

The final decision to make is about spine labeling. Most binders offer at least white, black, and gold foil stamping. Generally speaking, it is best to use white lettering. This shows up best in the stacks—especially if the stacks are not well lit. Black is a better option for some lighter-colored materials where white does not provide as good of a contrast. Some libraries choose gold because it is traditional, but gold can be difficult to see on some lighter-colored cloths and is often difficult to read when there is not direct light on the spine of the book.

In addition to the color of the stamping, it is important to give careful consideration to the amount of text you want to appear on the spine. Too much information can be as troublesome as not enough. As a general rule it is best to include both the title and the author on the spine with a space between the title and the author. Shorten the title if necessary so that too much of the spine is not covered in type. The titling decision is important for all bound items, but it is especially important for bound journals and magazines. The spine should contain information that will help the patron easily find the needed item. For journals, volume number and publication year should always be included in addition to the title. From there, it is important to know how the journal is indexed in order to know if issue numbers or page numbers also need to be included on the spine. Again, be careful not to overload the spine with information, and leave room between the title, volume, year, and other information to make it easy for patrons to identify the volumes they want.

Commercially bound volumes can be rather stark and utilitarian looking, but they can also look neat and orderly when all the volumes of a journal title on a shelf are bound in the same color with matching spine information. All library binders have the ability to match this information and will provide you with assistance and training on how you can keep track of the binding patterns for your various magazines and journals. Ask your binder for details.

Commercial binding is not the answer for every damaged volume. Sometimes it is more cost effective to simply replace the volume. Sometimes it is better to repair them. And ever more often in the digital age volumes are being withdrawn as the information becomes available electronically. But always remember that after a volume has been properly commercially bound it is very unlikely that it will *ever* require another preservation treatment. Few other preservation options can offer such a promise.

Note

1. Brian J. Baird, "Pioneering the Use of Polyurethane Adhesive in Library Binding," *Serials Librarian* 61, no. 2 (Spring 2011): 275–82.

Chapter 7

In-House Book Repair

In general, in-house book repair is one of the least effective and most inefficient forms of preservation, and yet it continues to be very popular. Book-repair workshops continue to be one of the most sought after training activities requested by small academic and public libraries. Book repair *can* serve an extremely important role in a library's overall preservation program but *only* if the repair staff is properly trained and properly equipped to perform repairs correctly and efficiently. Unfortunately, proper book-repair training can be expensive and difficult to obtain. There are many one- or two-day workshops that are offered throughout the country, but these courses do not generally provide the skills needed to evaluate damaged materials and diagnose the proper treatment in the context of the library's overall preservation and collection-development goals.

If a library has a commitment to establishing a book-repair program, it is important to get repair staff properly trained to perform various book-repair treatments. It is also vital that staff members are trained *how* to select the appropriate repair technique to use on a damaged item and when it is best *not* to repair an item in-house. A vital part of the decision-making process involves learning to evaluate the cost-effectiveness of the treatments being performed and the other options available. Even at minimum wage, it does not take very long before the time and materials spent on performing a book repair cost more than having the title rebound or replaced.

There are some strong advantages to having a good in-house repair program. An in-house program enables the library to repair items on a rush basis, quickly returning them to circulation. Also, an effective in-house repair program allows greater flexibility in what can be preserved. There are many times when damaged items would be lost if not for effective book repair where individual attention can be paid to damaged volumes.

Many book-repair manuals have been published throughout the years. Some are even available online such as the Dartmouth Preservation Department manual on book repair (http://www.dartmouth.edu), the Indiana University Preservation Department manual (http://www.indiana.edu), and the Alaska State Library manual (http://library.alaska.gov). Many of these manuals are well written with excellent illustrations and videos that help guide you through the described treatments step by step. However, when consulting these manuals it is extremely important to understand the audience for whom the manual was written. Many of the better manuals were prepared with research libraries in mind. Some of the treatments described in these manuals will be useful for public or small academic libraries, but most will not. Again, careful assessment is the key. Your library must determine what kind of in-house book repair it needs, how much support in terms of personnel and financial resources the library can afford, and the cost-effectiveness of the various treatments you plan to offer.

There are certain simple treatments every library should know how to handle such as simple paper mending, tipping-in loose pages, and tightening loose joints on a cover. From there each library must decide if it needs a greater range of treatment options such as spine repairs or even recasing books. The following pages will describe some basic treatment options complete with step-by-step instructions and some assessment aids to help you decide if the treatment is right for your library. However, before we begin with the specifics there is some general conservation theory that should be covered to provide some context to the following treatments.

The first rule of conservation is to not harm the treated item. Therefore, every treatment performed must not only extend the life of the item but also be reversible. This means being able to easily remove the materials used in the repair. The implication for these rules is that the materials used in the repair are nondamaging—meaning they will not damage the item over time by introducing harmful chemicals. It also means the materials will not become stiff or brittle over time. Finally, it means that adhesives used are generally reversible so that the repair materials can be removed. A great deal of time and energy has been dedicated to developing sound conservation materials for use in book repair. There are several reputable vendors who supply sound, conservation-grade materials for use in book repair. Unfortunately, there are also many vendors who sell supplies for use in book repair that are extremely damaging and harmful to your collections. It is not always easy for an untrained person to tell the difference. There was an ANSI/NISO standard, Z39.77-2000, entitled, "Guidelines for Information About Preservation Products" that has since become inactive but is still available from the National Information Standards Organization (NISO). This standard can help you identify terms that will ensure you are acquiring conservationally sound products. Make sure that the vendors you buy from are familiar with this standard and that the descriptive terms they are using for their products are in compliance with this standard.

In addition to the quality of the materials used in the book-repair treatment, it is also extremely important to only perform treatments that will not damage the item being repaired. Library conservators face several unique challenges not faced by other kinds of conservators. Books are not like other objects of art or historical significance. Books are three-dimensional objects designed and collected for the purpose of being used by readers. The conservation or book-repair treatments used in libraries have to be designed in a way that allows continued use of the damaged volume.

Over the centuries bookbinding techniques have evolved. Some of these changes have been good, but most have been designed to save costs rather than producing a product that will last a long time. Therefore, book repair involves more than simply learning a few techniques. It also involves knowledge of book structure; the physics involved in how a book functions, including the stresses experienced by a book as it is used; and the attributes of the different kinds of binding structures. This sounds involved, and it is, but at the same time it is not rocket science. To produce effective book-repair results, a person needs good hand skills—which can be learned; strong assessment skills—which this book teaches; and experience—which only comes from doing. The key point is that book repair is not a throwaway activity. Too many libraries fall into the trap of assigning volunteers or problem staff to perform book repairs in an out-of-the-way corner with little supervision. Book repair requires a lot of thought and care if it is going to be done properly—meaning, done in a way that will benefit the library.

Keeping the above context in mind, we will proceed to discuss a few basic book-repair techniques. In this book the highest level of treatment that will be presented is a spine repair. Other, more advanced treatments are possible, but most of them require a library to commit to a significant amount of supplies, equipment, tools, and the space to store them. They also require a significant increase in staff commitment. Generally speaking, most small academic and public libraries need the ability to perform some simple, stopgap repairs to extend the life of damaged items until they can be replaced or sent for rebinding. With the relatively inexpensive costs of library binding, it does not take very long before an in-house repair is more expensive than a new commercial binding.

Paper Mending

Heavily used library collections—especially children's collections—require a lot of paper mending. The important thing to remember about paper mending is that you are mending a page that is designed to be flexible, and therefore you *do not* want to introduce a mend that will greatly reduce the paper's flexibility. Pick up a book, turn the pages one at a time, and carefully examine how each page flexes and moves as the book is used. Even the pages that are not being turned are forced to flex. Placing a mend in a book that does not allow the page to flex as it did before will introduce stresses into the book that will promote future damage. Maintaining this flexibility involves two things: *what* mending materials are used and *how* they are employed.

Book and paper conservators favor using flexible, strong, Japanese handmade papers and water-soluble, wheat starch paste to perform their mends. The results are a strong, flexible mend that generally blends in well with most papers. Furthermore, the mend is reversible if it ever needs to be removed for some reason. Paper mending with Japanese paper and paste is a challenging process that takes a great deal of practice to perfect. Furthermore, the papers are expensive and wheat starch paste is difficult to prepare and does not store for very long without getting moldy or losing its adhesion qualities. Therefore, small academic and public libraries will generally want to opt for some ready-made mending materials available on the market.

There are several kinds of paper-mending materials on the market that do an adequate job. However, there are many more products sold that are damaging to paper. The general rule to remember for paper mending is that you want a product that is flexible and will remain so over time. You want a product that will not yellow or shrink over time. The adhesive used should not ooze over time, or dry up and come loose. The adhesive should not cause the paper to become translucent or cause inks to bleed or feather over time.

There are, primarily, two kinds of adhesives available in high-quality mending tapes—heat-set adhesives and pressure-sensitive adhesives. The heat-set tapes use a dry, heat-activated adhesive that bonds well to papers when applied with a heating iron. Heat-set tapes and tissues work well on many kinds of paper. Because the adhesive is dry there is less chance of the adhesive cross-linking with the paper fibers over time. There is also less chance of the adhesive causing inks to bleed, or for the adhesive to ooze. Oozing refers to the fact that acrylic pressure-sensitive adhesives do not dry out over time. This is good because it means the tapes will not dry up and fall off. However, it also means that the adhesive remains fluid, and if the proper type of mending tape is not used the adhesive can ooze out from under the tape over time, or be absorbed into the paper being mended, causing it to become translucent.

The problem with heat-set mending materials is that using these tissues and tapes can be fussy and time consuming. Furthermore, one runs a risk of damaging the paper with the heating iron. Heat affects different papers different ways. Some papers can withstand a great deal of heat; others will not. This is especially true of older papers. Generally, older papers burn much easier than newer papers.

Another concern is that many of the inks used in modern printing are heat-activated toners similar to those used in photocopying machines. The result is that over time small amounts of the ink from the pages will get deposited on the heating iron. It is important to make sure that the heating iron is kept clean—especially when using it for the first time after it has been turned on. If not, your mending efforts could result in unattractive dark smudges on the paper you are trying to mend.

Acrylic adhesive tapes employ a pressure-sensitive adhesive that readily adheres to most papers. A good-quality mending tape may appear to look and work like adhesive tape, but it is not the same thing. A good-quality mending tape is made of nondamaging materials that resist yellowing and oozing over time. In addition to using higher-quality materials, good mending tapes are also made of materials that are thin and flexible and will not impede the natural function of the mended page. The good-quality tapes employ a thin film of adhesive that results in reduced chances for oozing or bleeding. Normal adhesive tape has much thicker plastic and much more adhesive on the tape than high-quality paper-mending tapes.

The NISO standard "Guidelines for Information About Preservation Products" can help you in identifying attributes of high-quality paper-mending tapes and tissues, but perhaps an even simpler way is cost. A high-quality mending tape is not cheap. A roll of mending tape can cost the same as a dozen or more rolls of inexpensive adhesive tape.

Mending with adhesive tape can be extremely tempting, but you must recognize the long-term effects of such a decision. The excessive amounts of adhesive will ooze over time. The adhesive or the tape itself will often yellow and stiffen over time depending on the chemical makeup of the materials used. Therefore, if there is even a chance that the item is going to be kept for more than just a few years it is best to use high-quality archival tapes. But that said, it is important to recognize that in today's libraries materials get weeded at a much more rapid pace than in the past, and for popular authors, where multiple copies of a new title are purchased and later many of them are weeded from the collection, it might be okay to make a quick, easy mend with adhesive tape. The key is to be thoughtful and purposeful about the decisions being made. Do not just do what is easiest and most expedient.

Step-by-Step Instructions for Paper Mending

The biggest obstacle to paper mending is that it looks as if it is easy and straightforward. In reality, paper conservators spend years learning to become effective at paper mending. When done properly, paper mending requires a great deal of care, patience, and skill. Most people are unwilling to commit the time and patience necessary to become effective at paper mending. Understand this, and if your library uses volunteers for this treatment, be sure to monitor their work carefully to ensure quality is maintained.

The following instructions and drawings will take you through the steps of paper mending. The first step is to evaluate the torn paper to determine what kind of paper it is and how the item flexes. This will help you in deciding how best to mend the page. Your mend should not reduce the flexibility or function of the paper. For example, it does not take very much mending tape—even thin mending tape—to reduce the flexibility of thin paper. Also, some mending tapes blend in better on different kinds of paper. For example, a paper-based mending tape works well on most papers, but it can be very unsightly on glossy paper—especially dark-colored paper. Knowing the kind of paper will help you choose the right kind of mending materials.

Next, make sure the torn parts of the paper are properly realigned and laying flat before you begin your mend. Paper generally tears unevenly in a scarfing manner (see figure 7.1). Few tears are truly perpendicular to the surface of the paper. Most tears occur at an angle so that when mending the page the two sides of the tear only properly align one way. It is very important to make sure all the edges line up properly *before* the mending material is applied.

Begin your mend from the start of the tear working toward the edge of the page. This is important because it will help ensure that the tear lines up correctly. If the tear is misaligned, even a little bit, it can cockle the paper and dramatically affect how the page functions.

Do not use too wide of a piece of tape. The thinner the width of the tape, the less it will impact the flexibility of the mended page. Generally, the tape does not need to be any wider than a quarter to three-eighths of an inch wide. Use scissors to cut the tape down to the desired width. This does take extra time, but it also saves on the cost of tape, because a roll will last much longer.

Most tears are not straight. The obvious temptation is to use a wide piece of tape to cover as much of the tear as possible in one easy step. Generally, this will not produce a pleasing result. Use short pieces of thin tape and mend the tear. Try not to bend the tape to follow the twists and turns of the mend. Instead,

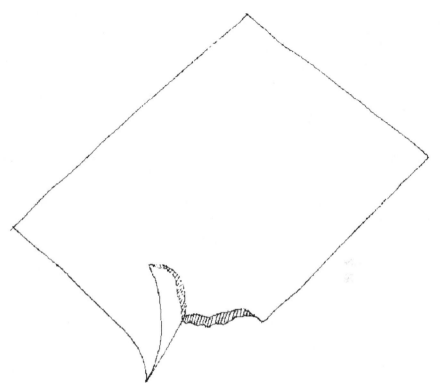

Figure 7.1 Picture of torn page showing scarfing

use several pieces of short tape as shown in figure 7.2. This takes more time, but it produces a better result. Try not to overlap the ends of the mending tape. These overlapping areas will cause extra stiffness and bulk.

Depending on the thickness of the paper and the nature of the tear, you may or may not need to mend both sides. If it is a small tear on thin paper, mending one side is usually sufficient. If there was a lot of scarfing when the paper was torn, if the paper is thick or heavily used, or if you are filling in a hole in the page, you will want to mend both sides of the page.

One final note on paper mending: Often, especially in children's books, multiple pages get torn in the same spot on each page. This can result in a rather large buildup in mending tape. Even a thin tape adds bulk, and if ten or more pages are mended you can start to feel the added thickness. If too much material is added to the book, it can add stress to the binding or the weakened pages that may cause future damage. Also, the added bulk of the mending tape can start to act as a hard edge against which the pages can become stressed or even

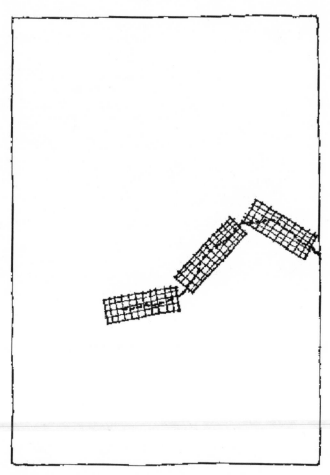

Figure 7.2 Properly mended tear where small strips are used

tear, similar to the hard edge on the top of a legal pad that is used to tear out the pages from the pad.

Tip-ins

All libraries face the challenge of reattaching pages into a book that have fallen out. This is particularly true for poorly produced, adhesive-bound items, missing pages replaced with photocopied pages, and inserted errata sheets. Like paper mending, tip-ins are not as straightforward or simple as they initially appear. However, it is important for every library to have at least one staff member who knows how to perform an effective tip-in.

The important thing to remember before performing a tip-in is that the finished treatment should not impede the normal function of the book. This means, *do not* use too much adhesive, and *do not* try to tip in too many pages into one spot. It is important that the adhesive is not allowed to ooze after the tip-in is performed and the book is closed. To demonstrate what I mean, take a small drop of water and allow it to drip onto a flat, smooth table; then slowly cover the drip with a piece of glass and see how much the water spreads out. If too much adhesive is used it can ooze out from the gutter into the pages and cause disastrous problems. Likewise, do not try to tip too many pages into a volume. Often huge sections will be torn out of a book or sliced out of a journal. As a general rule, never tip in more than fifteen adjoining leaves into a volume. Tipping in too many adjoining pages into a volume can cause a natural breaking point that will eventually cause the binding to fail.

To perform a tip-in, make sure there is a clean, straight edge where the item will be tipped back into the volume. If you are tipping in a replacement page or errata, trim the gutter edge to the proper size before gluing it in place.

Using strips of waste paper, mask off all but about one-eighth of an inch of the inner margin of the sheet to be tipped in (see figure 7.3). Brush a thin layer of polyvinyl acetate (PVA) onto the sheet, and then place it in the book where it belongs in the volume. Two tips: First, work quickly. After the page has been glued the thin adhesive dries quickly. Also, the moisture from the adhesive will

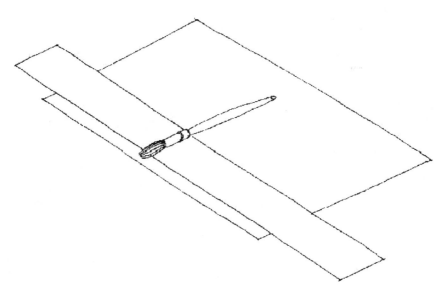

Figure 7.3 Page being masked off and glued prior to tipping it in

cause the page to begin to cockle and warp, making it hard to adhere into the book in a pleasing manner. Second, be careful how you position the glued page into the book. If care is not taken, it is easy to smear adhesive onto other pages, causing them to stick together.

Generally, it is best to work with the book laying open as flat as it can and to then place the page being tipped into the book so that the glued edge of the page is facing up (see figure 7.4). This will allow you to position the page without running as much risk of smearing PVA in places you do not want it to be.

When tipping in multiple pages, it is best to adhere the pages together first and to then tip the complete set of pages into the book. If there are only two or three pages to tip together, it is usually easiest to simply mask each page as described above and then tip them together.

If there are several pages that need to be tipped together, an easy trick is to line the pages up and to hold them together on the front edge of the pages using a bulldog clip or paper clips (see figure 7.5). Fold the pages back over on top of themselves, mask them off, and use a brush to spread adhesive on the exposed inner margin edges of the pages. Quickly fan the pages the other direction and repeat the step. Squeeze the pages together with your fingers or a bone folder and then tip them into the book.

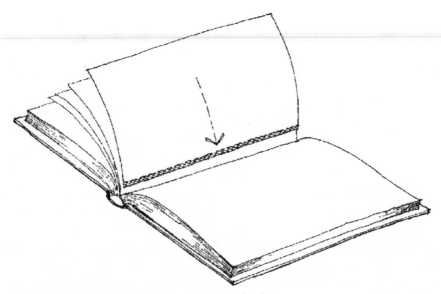

Figure 7.4 Proper way to place a tip-in into the book

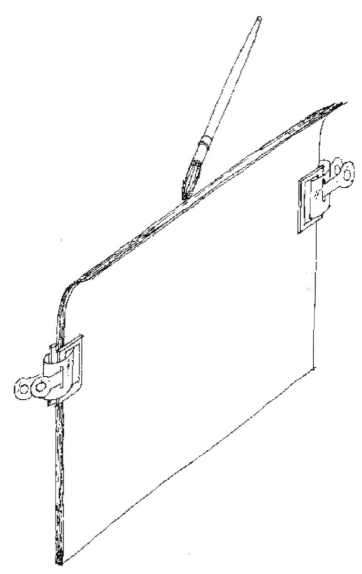

Figure 7.5 How multiple page tip-ins can be glued out at the same time

After the tip-in is complete, close the book and leave it closed under five to ten pounds of weight for at least ten to fifteen minutes. It is a natural inclination to want to reopen the book immediately to see if the mend worked as you intended it to, but doing so will weaken the PVA bond between the text block and the tipped-in pages. Therefore, it is best to wait until after the book has been pressed for several minutes.

After the book has been pressed, open it carefully to examine the effects of your repair. For all repairs that you perform it is important to take a little time and carefully evaluate the effect of the treatment. Check to see if the page is glued into place properly and how the tipped-in page functions. Look to see if any adhesive accidentally got on other pages and caused them to stick together. A good tipped-in page should function like all the other pages in the book. If too much glue is used, or if the glued-out area of the page was too large, it will be obvious. If patrons open a book and see a tipped-in page that does not function like the other pages because it looks as if it is stuck to the page next to it, they will automatically try to pull the pages apart. It is a normal, human reaction. It is, therefore, very important to perform your tip-ins—and other repairs—in ways that will not invite people to pick at the mend and cause more damage.

For replacement pages that are larger than the original pages of the book, you can trim them down to size before tipping them in, but generally you get better results by trimming them after the pages are tipped in. Insert a cutting mat, or thin, dense binding board under the pages that need to be trimmed. Use a scalpel or other sharp cutting tool to trim the pages down to the exact size of the original pages. Use light pressure on the cutting tool, and make several cuts as needed to cut through the pages. This takes a little practice, but soon you will become accustomed to the hand skills needed to perform this task cleanly.

Hinge Tightening

Many public libraries use dust-jacket covers for their hardbound books. As said before, these covers provide excellent support and protection for both the dust jacket and the book. Libraries with lots of dust-jacket covers have relatively few volumes that develop damaged spines, but the downside is that these books often develop loose hinges.

Patrons and, unfortunately, many library staff members remove books from the shelves by pulling on the headcap of the binding. The result is damaged spines. The plastic dust-jacket covers protect books from this damage by transferring the stress from the spine to the front boards of the book. The result is loose hinges (see figure 7.6).

Loose hinges can lead to future, more serious damage, and treating loose hinges is relatively quick and easy. Therefore, it is a good preventative repair that can reduce rebinding costs.

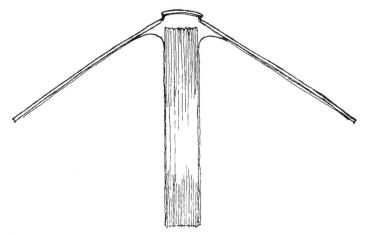

Figure 7.6 Example of book with loose hinges

Hinge tightening is performed by using a small glue brush or a knitting needle dipped in PVA to place adhesive into the inner joint area of the binding. This is done by standing the book up with the cover opened wide. The pages of the text block are also fanned out a bit to create as much space in the spine hollow as possible. Carefully slide the brush, or knitting needle with glue on it, into the hollow of the spine, and apply adhesive to the exposed joint area (see figure 7.7).

It is extremely important that no adhesive is allowed to get onto the spine of the text block. Doing so will cause the spine of the case binding to adhere to the spine of the text block. This will place strain on the case and the text block, and will eventually cause permanent damage.

Spine Repair

The benefit of using a spine-repair treatment, when it can be used, is that it is an effective and relatively inexpensive repair that results in a dramatic improvement to a book's strength in its most vulnerable areas—the joints and spine. This treatment replaces the damaged spine of a volume (see figure 7.8), allowing the original spine piece to be reincorporated into the binding if the titling is still legible.

Additionally, the text block is tightened back into the case when the new spine cloth is pressed into the joints of the case. A spine-repair treatment can be used as a stopgap measure to allow heavily used books to be repaired and quickly returned to circulation.

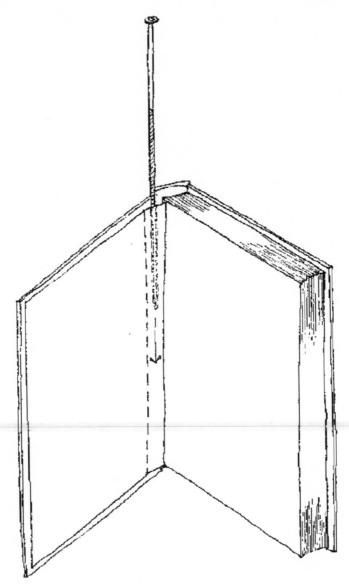

Figure 7.7 Example of glue being applied to loose joints

Spine repairs are very durable and will typically outlast an original publishers' case binding because the thin cloth or paper used in the original cover is replaced with strong book cloth. Spine repairs can serve as a permanent alternative to full rebinding if future use is not expected to be heavy. Spine repairs also

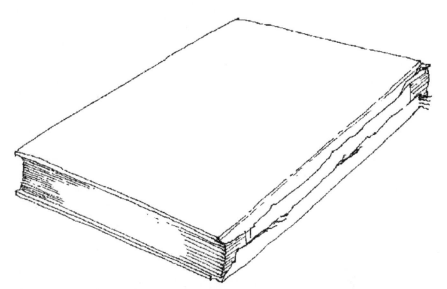

Figure 7.8 Example of book with damaged spine

allow the repaired books to retain the aesthetics of their original publishers' bindings. Furthermore, the repair poses no problem if, in the future, the volume needs to be commercially rebound, provided the spine-repair method used does not introduce adhesive tape or cloth onto the pages of the text block.

Candidates for a spine-repair treatment are characterized by a torn or flapping spine piece resulting from use, poor shelving practices, book return damage, and intrinsically weak publishers' binding materials. Spine-repair treatments are typically applied to publishers' case bindings where one or both of the outer hinges are torn, but the inner hinges of the endpapers remain undamaged.

Spine repairs are the most sophisticated repair treatment covered in this manual. It is a treatment that every library can use from time to time when circumstances require, but depending on your library's labor costs, such repairs may be more expensive than commercial binding. This is something each library has to determine for itself. However, there are times when the need for an immediate repair outweighs the cost difference. For example, there are many reference-type works that receive too much use for a library to feel comfortable about allowing one of these books to be gone for a month to the bindery. Therefore, knowing how to perform a spine repair is an important skill to have in your preservation toolbox.

A damaged spine is one of the most common types of damage in any library. Often many librarians wrongly assume that a damaged spine is simply an aesthetic problem, but a damaged spine frequently results in further, more permanent damage. Once the spine becomes damaged, there is a relatively short time before the boards of the case begin to work loose and fall off. Therefore, it is important to perform spine repairs as soon as the spine is damaged rather than waiting for the book to receive a few more uses. If you wait too long, the binding will be too damaged for this repair, and rebinding will be the only option.

Spine repairs only work under certain conditions. First, the book has to have a hardbound, case-binding structure with a hollow spine, meaning the spine piece of the cover is not adhered to the spine of the text block. Nearly all hardbound books printed over the last hundred years fall into this category. Second, this treatment only works on books with strong inner joints. If the board is loose, or the inner joint of the case binding is damaged, a spine repair will not work. Finally, this treatment can be used on any sized book, but generally, it is most effective when it is used on books no larger than two inches thick. This repair should also not be used on rare materials from a library's special collections. For these items a conservator should be consulted.

Performing a spine repair is not technically difficult, but it often requires hand skills that most people have not developed. Therefore, learning to perform this treatment usually requires both learning the steps of the treatment and training your hands to work in ways that are new and unfamiliar to you. *Do not get frustrated by this.* After practicing on five to ten books, most people become quite comfortable with this repair, and they learn to perform it in about thirty minutes.

Unlike the other treatments described earlier, spine repairs require a library to stock a modest supply of materials and tools. Purchasing these tools and supplies will cost a library about $150 depending on the tools and amount of supplies purchased. Before making this decision, it is best for library staff to take stock of their preservation priorities and decide if they want to make the commitment to the supplies, tools, and the staff time necessary to perform this treatment.

At a bare minimum, a library must have the following supplies on hand to perform a spine repair. Other tools and pieces of equipment can be purchased to make this repair easier to perform, and I will mention some of these in the treatment steps, but to begin with a library must as least have the following:

Sharp scissors
Bone folder
High-quality, one-inch-wide artist's paintbrush

Ruler
Sharp knife
PVA
Book cloth
Pressboards
At least ten pounds of weight

A word or two about tools: Purchasing high-quality tools and materials is important because inexpensive brushes, scissors, or glue will produce inferior treatments and cause the person performing the treatments a great deal of frustration. It has been my experience that high-quality tools pay for themselves over time as long as they are properly cared for and maintained. Inexpensive, low-quality tools need to be replaced much more often. Poor-quality scissors dull quickly, poor quality brushes lose their bristles and the ferrules rust, and low-quality knives rust or break.

In addition to purchasing high-quality tools and materials, it is also important to properly care for the tools you own. Too often people do not properly clean their glue brushes, and they return the next day to find a brush so stiff and inflexible that it cannot be used again. Through proper care, a high-quality paintbrush can be used for years. The key to caring for most tools is to keep them clean. When a brush is not being used, keep it in water so the adhesive does not dry in the bristles. After PVA has dried in the bristles of a brush it is impossible to remove it. Each day, after the brush has been used, wash it thoroughly with mild liquid soap (like dishwashing soap), being certain to rinse it completely. Then thoroughly dry the brush and shape it before leaving it to air dry.

Keep bone folders, knives, scissors, and other tools clean and dry. Do not let metal tools air dry. Doing so will facilitate rust or corrosion. It does not take long before tools can become quite dirty from residue adhesive, so clean them often and store then neatly. Some tools, like bone folders, knives, scissors, and rulers, can be damaged by the way they are stored. If all the tools are thrown into a drawer or box where they can bang into each other, then there is a risk of nicks and dull spots developing on blades and bone folders chipping.

Libraries dedicating a significant amount of staff time to book repair may wish to purchase some additional tools. Gaylord, University Products, and Talas have archival catalogs in which they sell many kinds of book-repair supplies and tools. These catalogs are nice because they have detailed, colored pictures of most of the products they sell, and they provide good written descriptions of the products they stock. Also, they sell tools and materials in small quantities. Start with the basic tool set, and then, based on time and experience, you can begin to augment your tool kit and range of supplies as needed. However, some key tools that prove useful are as follows:

Self-healing cutting mat
Scalpel and blades (or small, snap-off-blade utility knife)
Microspatula
Tweezers
Jeweler's pliers
Small, sharp-tipped scissors
Additional weights of various sizes
Book press

Some of these items can be rather expensive. A good self-healing cutting mat can cost over fifty dollars, but inexpensive ones cost under ten dollars. If you do not use it a lot, and take good care of it, a less expensive mat might do, but like most things, you get what you pay for. Book presses can cost several hundred dollars. Others items on this list are not very expensive, but they do prove handy to have around.

Step-by-Step Instructions for Spine Repair

The repair begins with removing the original spine piece and the cloth that makes up the joints of the cover. Using the boards of the cover as a cut-against, cut away a tiny edge of the old cloth, pressing firmly against a metal straight edge and making multiple light passes with a scalpel or utility knife (see figure 7.9).

The cut should extend one-eighth of an inch onto the board from the joint. Be very careful not to let the scalpel slip into the joint of the book because that would damage the inner paper hinge of the endpapers. Cut the cloth free on both sides of the book, and remove the cloth from the spine and joints of the book. Sometimes the cloth will still be adhered into the joint area of the book. Save the old spine so it can be reapplied if possible.

After the cloth is removed, the joints need to have all the old cloth and adhesive removed from them leaving a clean surface for the new cloth. Be careful when removing this cloth and adhesive to avoid damaging the gauze-like material called crash or mull that holds the text block to the case.

If the text block and pastedowns have begun pulling away from the boards (as with hinge tightening), reglue the crash and pastedowns to the boards using PVA (see figure 7.10).

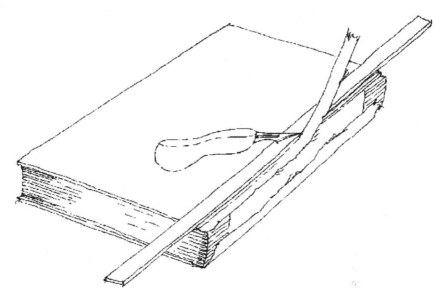

Figure 7.9 Example of spine being removed from book

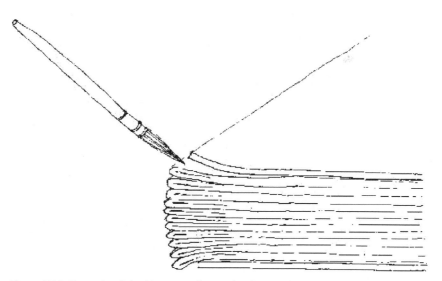

Figure 7.10 Example of the hinge area being glued

With the old spine removed, the book is ready to receive new spine cloth. With a pencil, draw a light line on the front board of the cover that runs parallel to the exposed back edge of the board to mark where the new piece of cloth will be glued to the cover. Continue the line around the edge of the board so it can be seen later when you need to mark the cloth for cutting.

Do the same thing on the back board of the cover. Figure 7.11 shows a three-quarter-inch spacer being used to make sure the line is parallel. A three-quarter- to one-inch-wide spacer is very useful and will be used a lot in this treatment. To prepare a spacer, simply cut a strip of binder's board that is three-quarters of an inch wide and about fifteen inches long.

This line will mark where the new spine cloth will be adhered to the book. Three-quarters of an inch is usually a nice standard width for the new spine cloth, but it is important to make sure that the new spine cloth does not cover titling information printed on the cover. So, if a piece of cloth three-quarters of an inch wide will obscure information on the cover, then decrease the area of the board that is covered.

Use a piece of flexible book cloth that is appropriately strong for the weight of the book being treated. Prepare it by squaring one edge using a straight edge and scalpel or on a cutter. Many book-repair supply vendors sell strong buckram cloth in rolls varying in width from two to four inches. The cloth should be

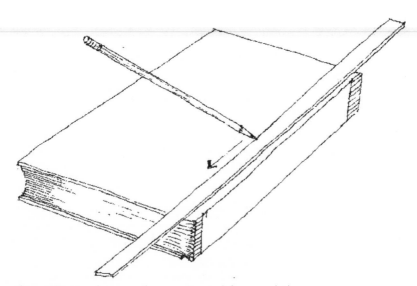

Figure 7.11 Line drawn on the cover to mark for new cloth

cut approximately two inches longer and two inches wider than the spine of the book.

When the cloth has been prepared, apply PVA to the area of the board from the pencil line to the edge of the board (see figure 7.12). Thoroughly coat the exposed paper in the joint area of the shoulder of the text block as well, *but not on the spine*. It is important to use enough adhesive to adhere the cloth to the book, but *do not* use too much adhesive.

If too much adhesive is applied it will ooze out at all the edges of the cloth, and when it dries it will make the joints of the books too stiff. Use a sheet of waste paper to mask off the book up to the line that was drawn to prevent PVA from getting onto the rest of the cover. Again, *be careful not to get PVA on the spine of the book*. The new cloth spine should not be adhered to the spine of the text block.

Once adhesive has been applied to the cover and joint, bone the new cloth onto the board and into the joint of the book so that the PVA adheres well. To avoid "shining" the cloth, bone it through a clean piece of waste paper.

With the cloth well adhered to the board and joint on the first side, wrap the cloth snugly around the spine of the book and bone it into the joint area on the

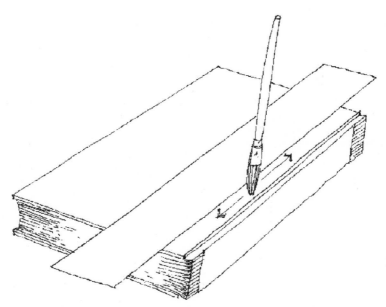

Figure 7.12 Glue applied to the area to be covered by the new cloth

opposite side. This is done to help form the new cloth to the spine and into the joint in preparation for cutting away the excess cloth.

With the cloth pulled tight around the spine, make marks on the cloth at the head and tail of the book that line up with the line drawn on the cover (see figure 7.13). The line that was drawn on the cover and extended onto the edges of the board should be visible with the book lying on top of the cloth. On a cutting mat, place a straight edge on the cloth so it bridges the two marks, and with a scalpel, cut away the excess cloth. This cut can be made carefully with scissors if you do not have a cutting mat and scalpel.

Using the three-quarter-inch wide strip, cut off the cloth at the head and tail of the book, leaving three-quarter's inch at each end for the turn-ins (see figure 7.14).

Tabs are cut to remove unneeded cloth from the turn-ins (see figure 7.15). The tabs are designed to be glued onto the pastedown with the center tab forming a headcap. A correctly shaped tab keeps cloth out of the inner hinge where it would restrict the movement of the board, while leaving enough cloth to cover the board up to the edge of the pastedown in the joint area. This turn-in will prevent the cloth from fraying at an exposed edge, and will give a nice finished look. The temptation is to cut out a triangle-shaped tab, but it is important to

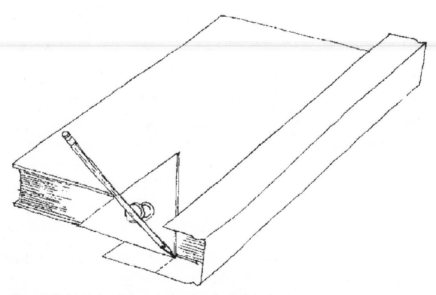

Figure 7.13 Mark the cloth at the head and tail of the book

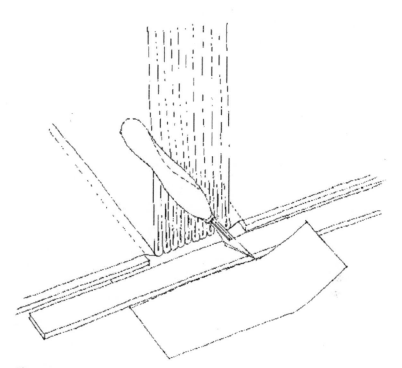

Figure 7.14 Trim the turn-ins at the head and tail of the book

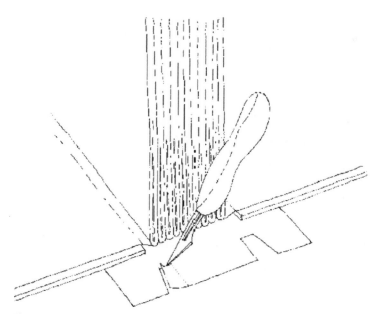

Figure 7.15 Tabs are trimmed for the turn-ins

square off the top of the tab nearest the book to form a trapezoid. This shape also helps prevent the new spine cloth from tearing easily.

On top of a cutting mat, hold the book on its spine with the boards laying open. With a scalpel, begin cutting the first tab. The first tab should be cut where the cloth has already been glued to the board. Cut the cloth at the point that lines up with the joint edge of the board and is far enough away from the top edge of the board to leave enough cloth to wrap up over the edge of the board and down to where the pastedown begins. Cut out toward the edge of the cloth at a slight angle so that the tab gets narrower toward the end. With some practice, the distance from the top of the book where the cut should begin will become easier to estimate. It is equal to the board thickness plus the distance from the pastedown to the top edge of the board. The second cut in the cloth is lined up with the edge of the shoulder of the text block and at an equal distance from the top edge of the board as the first cut. Again, taper the cut so that the center tab will be narrower at the end. Make a cut in between the two previously made cuts so the small area of cloth can be removed. These cuts can be made with scissors if you do not have a scalpel.

Cut all four of the tabs at the same time (see figure 7.16). When cutting the tabs, be sure that the part of the cloth that is not yet glued to the board is in the correct position before the tabs are cut. When the cover is opened, the cloth will have a tendency to shift. If the shift is not corrected the cutouts will not line up properly with the joint. An easy way of making sure the cloth is lined up properly is to make certain the scored mark on the cloth that was left from boning the cloth into the joint lines up with the joint. Glue the turn-ins to the inside of the board *only* on the side of the book that has already had the cloth glued to the outside of board (see figure 7.17). Be careful not to get too much adhesive on the cloth or it will ooze out and stick the endpapers together.

Next, glue the center tab in place. When done properly, the top of the new spine piece should lay in the same plane as the book cover. This seems logical enough, but it can often present a problem for people without a lot of experience—especially when performing spine repairs on thicker volumes. With the turn-ins on the spine completed, the cloth is ready to be glued to the other board.

Over a waste sheet apply glue to the strip of cloth, from the scored mark that was created when the cloth was boned into the joint to the outer edge, including the two tabs. Be sure not to get any glue onto the area of the cloth that will cover the spine of the book. Bone the cloth firmly onto the board, and into the joint of the book. Again cover the cloth with a waste sheet when boning it down to prevent shining the cloth. Bone the cloth so it adheres well to the book cover

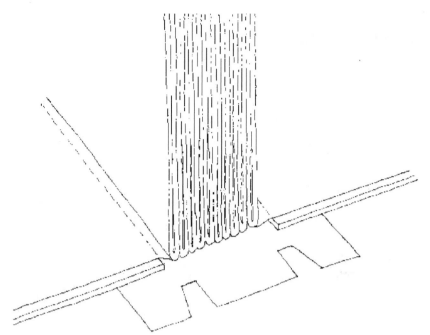

Figure 7.16 Close-up of how the tabs should be trimmed

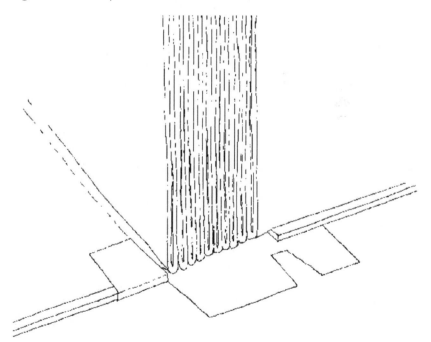

Figure 7.17 Turn-in and headcap are glued into place

before you bone in the joint area. This will ensure that the cloth lines up evenly on the board of the cover, and it will also help pull the cloth tight around the spine of the book.

Open the board, and make the last two turn-ins. Shape the head and tail caps with a bone folder so there are no irregularities in their shape.

With the new spine cloth in place, the spine repair is ready to be pressed (see figure 7.18). Place the book between pressboards, and place at least ten pounds of weight on the top board. Use a book press or standing press if one is available. Metal-edged pressboards are helpful because they help force the cloth into the joints of the cover. If you don't have pressboards with a metal edge, plastic rods or knitting needles can be placed into the joint area of the spine repair during pressing to produce a nice finished result.

If you are performing multiple spine repairs at one time, they can be pressed together by stacking them up with the largest books on the bottom and the

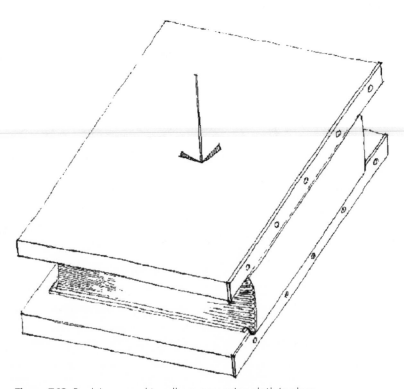

Figure 7.18 Book is pressed to adhere new spine cloth in place

smaller ones on top. A pressboard should be placed between the books to set the joint. The stack of books should form a pyramid. This will help ensure that books receive even pressure. Books should also be stacked alternately, with every other spine facing the opposite direction. Press the books for at least two hours, and preferably overnight, to allow the glue time to dry thoroughly.

After the book has been pressed, the four corners of the boards can be consolidated if they are damaged. Using a microspatula, apply PVA between the layers of delaminated paper that make up the board (see figure 7.19). When these delaminated layers and the outer layer of cloth are glued, pinch the leaves together to squeeze out the excess PVA and to shape the board. Allow the book to dry on top of some wax paper or silicon release paper for a couple of hours. Alternately, for a firmer repair, wrap a piece of wax paper or silicon release paper around the corner to act as a barrier sheet, place a piece of binder's board

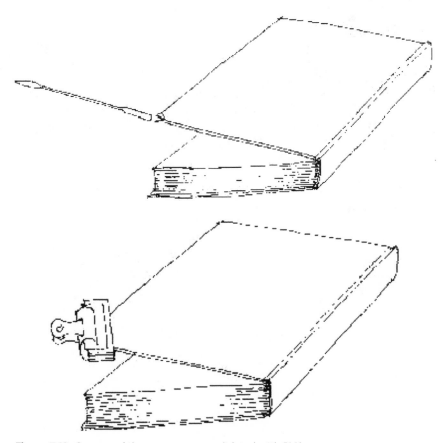

Figure 7.19 Corners of the cover are consolidated with PVA

on either side of the cover's corner, and apply pressure for a few hours with a bulldog clip (see figure 7.19). Before beginning this repair, it is a good idea to trim off the loose threads from the frayed edges of the damaged cloth. This will make the repaired corner look cleaner and neater.

If the original spine cloth is still legible, it can be adhered to the repaired spine to provide labeling information. Leather spines or plastic materials can be problematic. This is because PVA does not adhere well to some plastics, and leather often dries out and flakes away if the item receives much use. When the original spine label cannot be reused, a computer-generated paper label can be produced to provide the title and author information (see below). To prepare the original spine piece for reuse, the paper linings from the back of the spine piece must be removed. This will ensure that the spine piece adheres well to the new spine cloth, and it will allow for maximum flexibility. Often, much of the paper can be removed with your fingers and a microspatula (see figure 7.20).

Paper that does not peel off easily can be softened by applying a little water to the back of the original spine piece and waiting for it to soften the adhesive. Apply enough water to wet the paper and swell the adhesive, but do not get the spine piece too wet. In the past, book cloths were generally stiffened with starch fillers that are water soluble, so if the cloth gets too wet the starch will dissolve and the color will bleed out of the cloth. Let the water do the work for you. When the adhesive has softened, you can easily remove the paper lining using a microspatula or a dull knife. Patience results in the old lining coming off the spine piece with little fuss. Forcing it can easily tear or stretch the original spine piece. Also, be careful not to scrape too hard or to get water onto the front of the spine piece. Original stamping and older, starch-filled cloths are easily damaged while the cloth is in a softened condition because of the water.

When the original spine piece is clean, it can be applied to the new spine-repair cloth (see figure 7.21). Place the book in a finishing press or between two weights so that its spine is facing up. It takes both hands to properly apply the original spine piece, so it is important to have the book held firmly in place while you work. Ensure that the head of the book is facing away from you so you get the spine piece placed on the book the right way. It can be extremely frustrating to ruin a spine-repair treatment by placing the label on upside down.

Trim the width of the spine piece slightly to remove frayed edges. Make the spine piece narrow enough so that when it is glued onto the new spine cloth it will be one-sixteenth of an inch from the edges of each shoulder. This will prevent the attached spine piece from being as susceptible to abrasion when the book is handled in the future. If it does not affect its visual qualities, trim the spine piece to the height of the text block rather than the height of the boards.

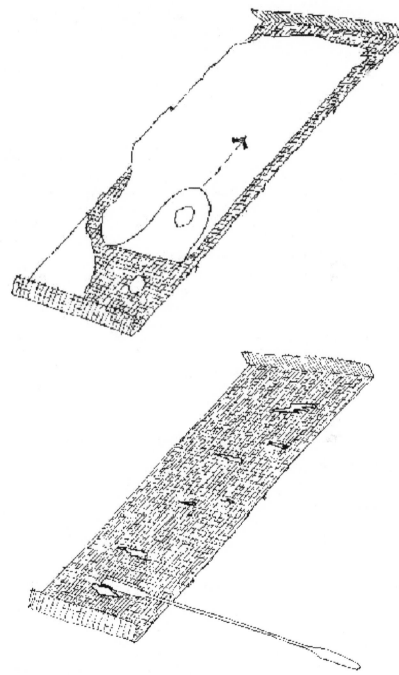

Figure 7.20 Lining is cleaned off of original spine piece

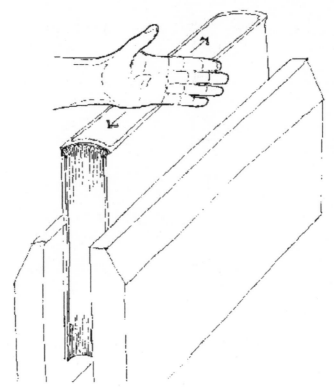

Figure 7.21 Original spine piece is applied to the new spine cloth

By shortening the spine piece to this length, the spine of the text block will help protect the original spine piece from undo stress that might cause it to delaminate. Finally, nick the corners of the spine piece with very small diagonal cuts; this will help prevent the spine piece from fraying.

When the spine piece has been trimmed, carefully apply PVA glue to it. Too much glue will cause oozing at the edges of the spine, while too little will leave bare spots that will not adhere. Be careful not to touch the glue-applied spine; fingers will remove the adhesive and leave a bare spot on the spine. How much glue you use depends a great deal on the kind of cloth used in the spine repair. Open-weave cloths are porous and can absorb a great deal of PVA. Coated cloths, like buckrams, absorb much less adhesive. Often, people use too little adhesive to apply the label. A general trick that helps you know if you have enough adhesive is to see how easily the glue-applied spine slides when it is placed on the spine of the book. If you have enough adhesive, you will be able to easily float the label around on the spine so you can line it up the way you want it. When placing the original spine piece, center on the spine of the book. Press the spine piece into place with the ball of the hand.

Cover the spine piece with a piece of wax paper or silicon release paper, and bone it very firmly for five minutes to ensure the adhesive has taken hold (see figure 7.22). Bone from the middle of the spine toward the four edges to remove any air bubbles. Bone the edges very well so they blend in with the spine cloth as much as possible, and so the spine piece will not pick or fray. It is very important to remember to apply your boning pressure down onto the spine. It is tempting to apply pressure in a sliding motion, which results in squeezing the adhesive out from under the label rather than forcing it *down* into the spine-repair cloth.

If your library plans to perform a lot of spine repairs, it is a good idea to purchase some spunbonded polyester material such as Reemay. This material has many

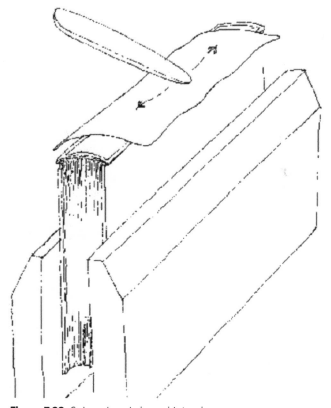

Figure 7.22 Spine piece is boned into place

excellent qualities. It is a malleable, fairly slick material that works well as a protection sheet when boning cloth. Also, it is translucent, allowing you to see what you are working on. This is particularly handy when boning labels onto spine-repaired books. It allows you to see quickly if adhesive is oozing out under the label before it has a chance to spread too far. Finally, spunbonded polyester has some attraction to PVA and will absorb some of the adhesive that might squeeze out from under a label being boned onto a spine.

If it is not possible to reuse the original spine, then it is fairly easy to produce a new, attractive label using a computer and printer. All modern word-processing programs have sophisticated graphics capabilities. This makes it easy to produce very functional attractive labels for your books. Simply measure the width of the spine with a ruler, and then produce a text box on your word-processing document to match that width. Most software packages give you the option of having a ruler displayed across the top of your document window. You have the ability to establish the measurements of the ruler to inches, centimeters, pica, and so forth.

Type the title and last name of the author into the text box. As a general rule, I try to make the text as bold and large as possible so it can be easily read by patrons. Generally, I will make the author's name a little smaller than the title and set it off from the title with a blank space.

Using a condensed typeface will help you produce nice-looking labels that are easier to read. In addition to the basic information, you may choose to add some border lines to the label as well. The idea of adhering a paper label to a finished book goes back hundreds of years. Take a look at how books were labeled through the years. With a little careful study you will soon recognize patterns and traditions that have carried on throughout the years. Implementing these traditions and patterns into the labels you produce will cause the labels you generate to look as if they belong on the books you have repaired as opposed to looking as if they were simply a typed title glued on as an afterthought. Figure 7.23 shows several examples of how a finished label could appear.

After the labels are generated, print them on a laser printer on acid-free paper. Do not use inkjet printed labels directly on the books. The ink in inkjet printers is water soluble, so they will run and smear if the label gets wet. Even a moist palm print can cause the ink to smear. Furthermore, many inkjet inks fade very quickly in the light, so in a few years the label will fade to a brown, then tan, and then it will disappear.

To further protect the label, spray the printed sheet with a coating of clear acrylic. This will help protect the label over time from abrasion and soiling. Be-

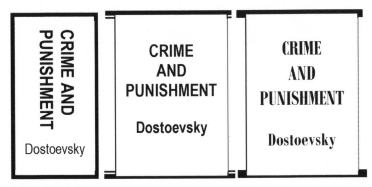

Figure 7.23. Examples of computer-generated labels. *Created by the author.*

cause of the organic solvents used in acrylic spray coatings, it is good to use a fume hood, or to spray the labels where there is plenty of ventilation.

When the spray coating has dried, you can cut the labels out and adhere them to the spine of the volume. For aesthetics, it is usually best to trim off the vertical lines on labels where the text runs horizontally as shown in figure 7.24. Labels with vertical text usually look better with a complete border.

Apply the label using the same directions as given above for reusing an original spine piece as the label.

Figure 7.24 Examples of trimmed computer-generated labels. *Created by the author.*

Chapter 8

Preservation Treatment Decision Making

It is difficult to know where in a preservation manual to place a chapter on treatment decision making. Treatment decision making is the first step undertaken on any preservation treatment being performed; however, it is difficult to discuss strategies for how best to treat an item if the treatment options have not previously been discussed. In many ways, the struggle of deciding where to place this chapter is typical of the treatment decision-making process. The first rule to remember for treatment decision making is that there are few hard and fast rules. The following pages and charts will provide some guidelines and strategies that will prove helpful in deciding how best to treat damaged materials, but as you begin applying these guidelines you will often find yourself holding a damaged volume that does not easily fit the guidelines provided. This happens because of the wide variability in volume structure, individual library policy and practices, and the preservation resources available.

Do not get frustrated when you find yourself uncertain on how best to preserve a volume. Take comfort in the fact that almost any decision you make will probably have some positive effect on the item or the collection. Do not allow yourself to become paralyzed by indecision. When in doubt, make a guess. A thoughtful, educated, conservative decision will rarely be wrong.

Treatment decisions involve many levels. There is always an economic aspect to every decision. For example, is it more cost effective for your library to discard the damaged item and replace it with a new copy? Is it less costly to rebind the item or have it repaired in-house? Experience and practice will help make these decisions easier, but the dilemmas will never completely disappear. However, one thing that can help you in the decision-making process is the information you gain from a careful collection and preservation assessment.

A policy for how your library will make treatment decisions must be based on the needs of the collection; the resources available, including funding, vendors, and staffing; and the collection-development policies of the library. For this reason, the decision-making flowchart presented below will not be the same for each library, and the final decisions reached in your library could be quite different from most other institutions, but the general decision-making process will need to follow the same basic steps.

Treatment decisions are most easily understood when viewed as a continuum with simple book repair at one end and single-item conservation treatment at the other.

There are many simple repairs such as tip-ins and simple paper mending that can be easily done in-house. The vast majority of materials in small academic and public libraries can be best handled by a commercial bindery if the volume is going to be kept in the library for an extended period of time, or if the volume is anticipated to receive a lot of use. On the other end of the continuum are higher-end book repair and single-item conservation treatment.

It does not take very much experience trying to determine how best to treat an item before you will understand why treatment decision making is best viewed as a continuum. Many decisions are easy, but things become less clear as they approach the line between the various treatment decisions. For example, spine repairs can fall into either end of the continuum depending on the resources of the library. For example, if a library has a qualified staff member who can perform spine repairs in an efficient manner, and if that library cannot obtain inexpensive library binding, it may be less expensive for that library to perform as many spine repairs as possible. For that library, spine repair will fall into the simple book-repair part of the continuum, and the amount of area on the continuum assigned to library binding will be smaller. By contrast, a library that has limited staff resources and a good binding contract may find it is cost effective to rarely perform spine repairs in-house and to instead send everything to the library binder. For this library, spine repairs would be a higher-end book-repair treatment reserved for those items that need to be rush repaired, or that have special needs that require them to be treated in-house rather than at a bindery.

Only through careful assessment of both the resources available to the library and its collection-development policy can a library decide where the lines fall

Simple	Library	Higher end	Single-item
Book	Binding	Book	Conservation
Repair		Repair	

Figure 8.1 Treatment decision-making continuum. *Created by the author.*

for them on their treatment decision-making continuum. Every library, regardless of size, faces the same challenge when grappling with its treatment decision-making policy. Every line on the treatment decision-making continuum represents a gray area where tough decisions need to be made. For this reason, the graphic is presented as a line with a gradated change in color to suggest the ambiguity involved with treatment decisions that fall close to the edges of each area on the continuum. Careful and continuous assessment is the only way to have confidence that you are making good treatment decisions that take into account the collection-development policy for the library, the needs of the collection, and the resources available both internally and externally. In other words, treatment decision making is always an evolving, learning process that is improved upon through experience and evaluation of the process.

In practical terms, treatment decision making is as much art as it is science. The best way to ensure that effective treatment decision making is taking place is to assign one careful staff member to do the job as part of his or her regular assignment. Over time this person will learn to juggle the many factors that impact each treatment decision in a quick, seamless manner. After a while this will become second nature to the staff member, and the person will only remember how involved the process is when trying to explain what he or she does to another person.

Essentially, the review process entails taking each damaged item through the following flowchart. When the decisions are hard other factors can come into play such as follows:

- How often does the volume circulate?
- How long will this item be kept in the collection?
- Will it be superseded by another edition in the near future?
- Is the item one of several copies owned by the library? If so, does the library still need all of its copies, or has use of the title dropped off enough to safely withdraw the damaged item without impacting access?
- Can the library afford to have the volume removed from access for several weeks while it is being rebound?

Answering these questions can help in the decision-making process when the answers to the questions on the flowchart are not clear cut. The flowchart showing in figure 8.2 is for a library that finds that spine repairs are generally less cost effective than library binding. This will probably be the case for most libraries. Therefore, for this example library, spine repairs are only performed under special circumstances. For another library, spine repairs may be more cost effective than commercial binding so its flowchart would look different.

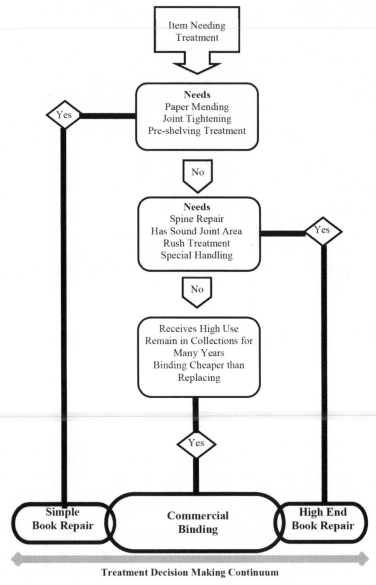

Figure 8.2 Treatment decision flowchart. *Created by the author.*

The important thing to remember is that you are trying to decide how best to preserve a book, and for the most part there are few wrong decisions. Almost any careful, well-thought-out decision will result in extending the life of the object in hand. The concern comes when you remember that you are making these decisions hundreds or thousands of times a year. For the individual book a bad choice may result in a book lasting twenty more circulations rather than a hundred more circulations if the correct decision had been made, but this is still twenty more circulations than the item would have had if no preservation treatment had been performed. However, if you repeatedly make a treatment decision that costs your library an extra two dollars per volume in either actual dollars or staff time, then you could cost your library hundreds or even thousands of dollars a year. This is why careful and continual assessment is important.

Robert Kaplan and David Norton developed an assessment tool called the Balanced Scorecard.[1] The essence of the Balanced Scorecard approach to assessment is that it looks at all levels of a business or organization. The Balanced Scorecard approach works well for preservation issues because preservation, when done properly, impacts all aspects of a library's operation. The Balanced Scorecard links performance measures in four areas: services provided; effectiveness and efficiency of daily operations; financial; and future planning and direction. In the electronic information age it is more important than ever to make sure preservation decisions take into account not only the physical needs of the item in hand but also the collection-development policy and strategic plans of the library. Unlike in the past, where individual libraries stood alone, modern libraries policies must take into account any consortia of libraries to which the library belongs. We talk about libraries without walls, and that reality impacts preservation decisions. Interlibrary loan, sharing of electronic information, and the changes in library-use patterns all effect collection-development policies and therefore preservation strategies.

A Balanced Scorecard assessment of preservation in a library would look at the performance measures illustrated in figure 8.3. The treatment decisions made on individual volumes encompass a wide range of information for many different areas. The Balanced Scorecard method recognizes that to have efficient and effective production it requires careful assessment of the entire library organization. It is for this reason that this manual takes such a broad view of preservation in a library. It recognizes that it is impossible to establish an effective preservation program without information about the collection-development policy, the budgetary restrictions in the library, the customer base served by the library, and the nature of its collections. Individual treatment decisions must also take this information into account. Again, this makes it sound like a daunting effort, but in truth, the human mind is an amazing thing, easily capable of learning to make treatment decisions based on multiple interrelated criteria.

Finally, a very important part of the treatment decision-making process is follow-up assessment. Have the staff members performing the book-repair

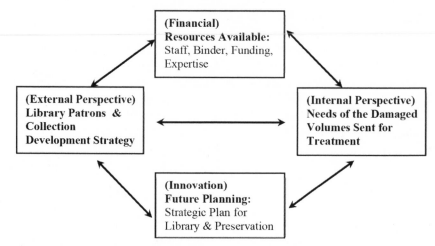

Figure 8.3 Balance Scorecard performance measures for preservation. *Created by the author.*

treatments time themselves occasionally to determine how long, on average, it takes to perform the various treatments. Evaluate the bindings that return from the commercial bindery to determine if items are bound well, in the correct colors, and following the directions given. Determine how long it takes for staff members to process materials for binding to determine what additional labor costs need to be factored into binding costs when making treatment decisions. Also, while evaluating damaged items sent for preservation treatment, pay close attention to those items that are returning for a second treatment. Try to determine why the first repair or library binding failed. If the previous treatment itself did not fail, determine if the treatment introduced pressure or stress on the binding that precipitated the damage you are now seeing. This kind of assessment will help ensure that the treatments being performed in your library are not introducing new problems that will cause future damage.

Networking

Those who are responsible for library preservation can benefit greatly from networking with others in the field who share similar experiences. Networking is important to any service-based profession, and library employees have been effective at establishing networks and professional organizations on both local and national levels. However, for most libraries, the people assigned to preservation-related activities usually do these tasks only as one part of their daily assignment. Therefore, when attending conferences or workshops, they most often tend to focus on their primary job assignments. As a result, there are few state or regional organizations for smaller-sized libraries that have preservation components. Many state library conferences will have one or two preservation-related workshops or presentations, but they do not offer discussion groups or roundtables where people interested in preservation can get together to discuss practical issues they face on a daily basis in their jobs. It is important to find ways of establishing these networks so you can learn from the experiences of others, and so you too can share your expertise. Professional preservation administrators have found networking to be invaluable in fulfilling their jobs, and part-time preservation people would also benefit from sharing with others.

Networking is important at all levels of preservation and can be useful in disaster-planning efforts, environmental monitoring, and assessment strategies. However, networking is included in this chapter because most people performing preservation activities in an academic or public library primarily focus their attention on providing preservation treatment for damaged items. Therefore, it is often on this topic that most people with preservation assignments value networking with their colleagues.

It is generally not that difficult to establish a forum for holding a preservation-related discussion at a state or regional library conference. The secret is to get started early. Do not wait until the conference is announced and the schedule is set. Check with the state library or the organizing agency to learn when the next conference will take place. This is often on their website. Talk to the person responsible for scheduling meetings, and then get a meeting set. Next, use electronic lists and newsletters to let people know about the meeting. Do not expect things to go too quickly. It may take a year or two for people to learn about the group and make time in their conference schedule to attend the session. It takes one or two people to provide the energy and dedication to get the group organized and kept alive until it gets enough momentum to carry itself. If you are responsible for preservation, you will find that it is time and energy well spent to work to establish a group of interested people to discuss preservation issues.

Note

1. Robert S. Kaplan and David P. Norton, *Translating Strategy into Action: The Balanced Scorecard* (Boston: Harvard Business School Press, 1996).

Chapter 9

*Training Staff and Patrons on Care
and Handling of Library Materials*

As mentioned in the second chapter of this manual, the most important preservation activities a library can engage in are preventative in nature. Chapter 2 talked about environmental monitoring because these efforts impact every item housed in the library. Another important preventative preservation activity is to train the staff and users on how to properly care for and handle library materials.

Think about the number of times the library staff handles an item before it reaches the shelves to be available to a patron. First an item is unpacked from the box it was shipped in, then it is processed by the acquisitions staff, and then again by the cataloging staff. Next, it receives library markings, a barcode, identification stamping or bookplates, and so forth. Finally, it may receive some kind of shelf-preparation treatment like a dust-jacket protector or paperback cover stiffener. The item is then sent to be shelved in the stacks by shelving staff members who usually handle the book at least twice before it reaches the shelf. If some of the processing is done by a library vendor or a service bureau, then the items must be unpacked and repacked, shipped to the library, unpacked, and then shelved.

Likewise, when an item returns from circulation it is repeatedly handled by the circulation staff and the shelving staff before it is placed on the shelf to begin the process over again. Every time a library staff member handles a book he or she has an opportunity to help preserve the item or to help destroy it.

For the library staff this means workflow procedures and habits. Library staff members handle dozens to hundreds of items each day. The processing procedures and habits used by each staff member could have serious effects on the life of the volumes being processed. The idea of book training was discussed earlier, but it applies to this chapter as well. When a book is new it should not be forced open too quickly or too far. The library staff should be trained to take the time and care to handle these items gently. Every book should be trained at least a little bit before it is passed through the processing units and placed on the shelf.

Following are some general guidelines that staff members should follow as they process library materials:

- In cold weather it is best to let the boxes of volumes received from the vendor, or the service bureau, acclimatize for about twenty-four hours before they are unpacked. This also applies to materials returning from the library bindery. Opening these boxes and processing the books inside could be very damaging to the materials. Cold adhesives are very inflexible, and too much handling at that time could cause the spines to crack or be damaged.
- Open the boxes carefully. Every person in charge of preservation treatment for a library has seen books enter his or her unit that have been accidentally sliced by a person opening a box of new acquisitions.
- Generally, it is the person opening the book for the first time who has the greatest potential to damage it. This person should be trained to treat the books with special care and take time to train the books a little so they will not be damaged by future processing and use.
- Most library processing involves reading information on the title page. New books, especially adhesive-bound books, do not want to lay open. All too often processing staff members are tempted to overbend the cover back to allow the book to lay flat. *Do not do this!* Instead, make sure the processing staff members have book snakes or other light weights to hold books open to the desired page. It is also important for these staff members to have sufficient work space to allow them to open the books they are processing without having to stack them on top of other materials.
- It is important to use nondamaging bookplates, barcode stickers, and other identification labels, and so forth. All paper products should be acid free, and stickers—if they must be used—should employ a non-yellowing acrylic adhesive.
- Do not try to carry too many books at one time or remove too many books from a shelf at one time. It is very tempting to try to remove many books from a shelf at one time by placing your hands on either side of the stack and using pressure and friction to keep the books together while you move them. This is very dangerous for the books because if one book slips it is like removing the keystone from an arch—the entire stack falls to the ground.
- Keep work areas tidy and well organized. This is important for many reasons. First, a tidy, well-organized work area will result in better, more efficient production. This is good for the library. It will also reduce the

amount of repetitive stress placed on staff members, which is good for their health. A clean, well-organized work area is more enjoyable to be in. It will contribute to a better work environment, which will impact employee satisfaction. A tidy work area will also affect the preservation of library materials. It will mean that there is plenty of space to work on the materials being processed. This will reduce the strain on materials.

- Develop proper strategies for moving materials around the library. Many library staff members develop bad habits for transferring materials on book trucks. Do not overfill book trucks. This is a common temptation—especially for the staff in charge of reshelving materials. An overfilled book truck represents many potential disasters. Overfilled trucks are heavy, and difficult to move, increasing the potential for tipping them over. They are unwieldy, and difficult to steer, increasing the potential for crashing them into doorways or shelving, which can cause severe damage to books. Do not make book trucks top heavy. This is a common temptation. The top two shelves of a book truck are most exposed and easiest to access, so they are often the only shelves used. The result is a top-heavy book truck that can easily tip over. Properly stack materials on book trucks. Again, it is tempting and easy to create several stacks of books on the shelves of the truck rather than taking the time to stand the books up straight. The result is that the piles slide against each other when the truck is moved, and eventually books start to fall off on the ground, causing damage.

- Shelve materials properly. It is often easier for the shelving staff to over-pack shelves with books rather than shifting the collections a little to provide the needed space. A walk through the stacks of many libraries will reveal areas that are badly overpacked and then other areas that have plenty of growth space. This problem has been exacerbated by the advent of electronic information. Not every subject area has equally adopted this technology, resulting in some subject areas (like the sciences) experiencing less shelf growth than others (like the arts and literature). Careful shifting can eliminate this problem, but it requires effort and time that some staffs and libraries are unwilling to commit. Materials should be shelved and supported so they stand straight on the shelf, with the spines of the books facing out. If a book is too tall for the shelf, shift the shelving when possible to provide the necessary space. Materials should be snug on the shelf so that each item provides some support to the items next to it, but they should not be packed so tightly that it is difficult to remove an item. A good rule of thumb is that a person should be able to remove a volume from the shelf without friction dragging the items next to it off as well. When the item is removed, there should be a hole left on the shelf to easily fit the volume back into place. If the hole disappears, the shelf is packed too tightly.

- Carefully examine the book returns used by the library. Nearly all book returns pose great potential for damage, but some are worse than others.

It is important not to have a book return that allows items too much of a free fall. Do not let book returns get overfilled. Empty outside book returns often—especially if they are exposed to direct sunlight. The inside of an enclosed book return—especially a metal one—can reach well over a hundred degrees even on a mild summer day. In the winter, these metal returns can be significantly colder than the outside temperature—especially for items left in the return overnight.

- Take time to examine materials returning from circulation to see how they are holding up to use. This is an important ongoing assessment of how well preshelving treatments, in-house repairs, and commercial bindings are holding up to patron use. This assessment time also enables the library to identify items in need of minor repair before the damage becomes so severe that it either cannot be repaired or cannot be repaired easily.

There are several good videos and web pages that can be useful to help train library staffs on the proper care and handling of library materials. The Library of Congress has some useful tips on their website. Kansas State University also has a practical five-minute training video on YouTube. And an entertaining video aimed at student users of the library was created by Brigham Young University and is also on YouTube.[1]

In addition to establishing good care and handling procedures for the library staff, it is also important to train library users to treat materials with care. Again, every time users handle a book they have the potential to help preserve it or help destroy it. By raising awareness of preservation issues, patrons learn how they too can help preserve the library's collections. This is important for more than just the obvious reasons. It helps in developing goodwill for the library, and all libraries can benefit greatly by having their constituencies think favorably of them. People are pleased when they see that their library is making an effort to preserve the materials they hold in their collections. It demonstrates that they are being responsible with their public trust. Such demonstrations result in favorable votes from college boards and city councils for additional funding in times of building renovations or other capital expenses. And in the electronic information age, when the public questions the need for libraries, it is especially important to demonstrate a strong stewardship of the library's collections and budgets.

There are several relatively simple things libraries can do to promote preservation efforts by their patrons. Posters, signs, and bookmarks have been effective and are available from several vendors and the American Library Association. It can also be very effective to develop your own posters or bookmarks by holding a contest for patrons to enter their design for the best preservation poster or bookmark. This can be effective because it raises awareness of the issues early in the process. It can also result in favorable press coverage to further educate the population about the preservation concerns of the library.

Useful signs and posters can be used to educate patrons about the proper use of photocopiers or scanners to prevent damage to materials while trying to copy them. If your library has book-edge copiers, make a sign demonstrating how book-edge copiers work and explaining why they are important. Do the same for book scanning equipment—especially if you have a top-down scanner that has a supportive book cradle. Such signs should appear at each copier and scanner. Other helpful signs and posters can explain about the dangers of food and drink in the library, explain the importance of patrons treating the materials they take from the library with care, and warn against mutilation of library materials. While at the University of Kansas Libraries, we developed a bookmark to help educate patrons about these concerns that was very effective. Other libraries have experienced similar success. The guidelines on the University of Kansas Libraries' bookmark represent some of the issues we felt patrons needed to know based somewhat on the results we gained from our condition survey. Libraries face difference issues, so your posters, signs, and bookmarks will need to be made to address your specific issues.

An effective way of educating users is to work with patron groups. College libraries can add preservation components to their general library orientation for new students. Public libraries can work with grade-school children and other groups to teach them how to care for library materials and why it is important. These initial introductions do not need to be long or complex. In just a few minutes it is easy to raise awareness in people's minds and plant seeds that will produce future benefits for the library.

Note

1. "Care, Handling, and Storage of Books," Library of Congress, accessed September 18, 2017, http://www.loc.gov; "Care and Handling of Library Materials," Kansas State University, YouTube, August 31, 2011, https://www.youtube.com; "The Many Stations of Book Preservation," Brigham Young University Library, YouTube, August 28, 2014, https://www.youtube.com.

Chapter 10

Disaster Planning

Being properly prepared to cope with a disaster can result in lives being saved and a high percentage of library materials being recovered. Experience has shown that the key to effectively coping with a disaster is an immediate and well-organized response to the situation. This is done by first ensuring the safety of individuals and then the protection of the collections during a disaster, followed by purposeful recovery efforts.

When writing a disaster plan begin with the premise that you are preparing for the worst thing that can happen, to happen, at the most inopportune time. Prepare your plan so it can help the brand-new staff member just hired to work at the circulation desk during off hours. These are generally college students or other young people working part time. They are not going to have the experience or training necessary to do a great deal of creative problem solving, so there needs to be a disaster plan in place that will help them through the crisis in a step-by-step manner.

Next, do not reinvent the wheel. There are many examples of very effective disaster plans that are available in print or on websites. There are also packages available that can help you easily create a disaster plan for your library by simply filling in the blanks they have provided with information relevant to your library such as the director's name and home number, the head of facilities management, and so forth.

Finally, when getting started, take a careful look at your library and determine the potential disaster risks that exist. For example, is your library in a flood plain, or in a low area where water will collect during a flood situation? What natural disasters, such as earthquakes, tornadoes, or hurricanes, occur in your area? There are many simple things that can be done to greatly reduce the risk of loss by disaster. Begin by carefully evaluating the condition of the library and the threats that are posed to it. For example, I consulted with one public library on its disaster plan. They worked hard and developed a very good disaster plan for their building, but they wanted me to review their work. The library was built in an old warehouse that had been very nicely remodeled into a comfortable, inviting library. Part of the remodeling effort had involved placing a large, curved, metal canopy over the entire collection. This was very effective in creating a nice reading space, but it also had an advantage that was unrecognized by the library staff. In the event of a water leak from the roof or from a broken water pipe overhead, the large canopy would act like a large umbrella over the entire collection. However, on a walk through the building, I noticed that many of the bookshelves for their reference collections were placed directly under the edge of the canopy. The effect would be like standing under the edge of a roof in a rainstorm. All the water would have been funneled onto these important—and expensive—reference works. By simply moving the shelves a few feet so they would be under the canopy, they were able to greatly reduce the potential for damage.

After the threats to your library have been determined, take stock of the resources available to help you respond to disaster. Meet with your local police and fire departments. Get to know these people—especially the fire departments personnel. These professionals have a vast amount of experience and training and can do more to help save your library and its collections in a crisis situation than any other organization. Educate the police and fire departments about your floor plans, your important collections, the risks that fire and water pose to your collections, and so forth. When you have finished your disaster plan, share it with the police and fire department to get their input.

Learn what services are available from your county or city or parent organization, and coordinate with them to ensure that no duplication of effort is taking place. This is especially true for electronic information and collections, and computer equipment. Most states or organizations have separate disaster plans for their computer networks established by information technology professionals.

Meet with your insurance agent and learn the details of your insurance policy. Make sure the agent understands the risks posed to your library collections from fire, water, smoke, and so forth. It is important that the insurance company understands the need to respond quickly in the event of a disaster and allows the library to retain the services of an effective disaster recovery firm when appropriate.

Understanding the potential threats to your library, and the resources available, will help you develop a useful and effective disaster plan. It will help you determine how to create the specific plan that you need. After this evaluation is finished it is time to begin preparing the document. Most regional conservation centers offer disaster-planning workshops on a regular basis. Their website (http://www.rap-arcc.org) will provide some useful information about workshops and other disaster-planning information. Also, Conservation OnLine (http://cool.conservation-us.org) has many examples of disaster plans and other useful information.

It will be talked about later, but a point to remember when looking at other disaster plans and templates is to remember to keep it simple. Make sure the plan is as detailed as it needs to be, but more is not always better. Do not let the important information get lost in a mountain of details.

Effects of Water, Fire, and Smoke on Library Materials

To be able to effectively cope with a disaster, it is important to understand the effects water, fire, and smoke have on the materials collected in most libraries. Nearly every type of disaster situation involves water of some kind. Floods, fires, tornadoes, hurricanes, and earthquakes can all result in water damage to the collections either as a direct result of the disaster or, for example, from broken water pipes caused by earthquakes or tornadoes. Therefore, it is important to know how water will impact the collections and how to effectively begin recovery operations. Smoke and fire are also major threats to library collections, and the effects of both need to be understood. Following is a brief discussion of the impact of these disaster risks on the various materials collected by most libraries.

Books and Paper

Books and paper make up the vast majority of most library collections in terms of physical space. Fortunately, books and paper are fairly resilient when it comes to withstanding most disasters faced by libraries. When proper disaster-recovery methods are followed, the vast majority of a library's books and paper collections can be recovered from fire, water, smoke, earthquakes, or other disasters. True, paper and books burn, but usually they do not burn very well because they are packed tightly on shelves or in filing cabinets where the paper cannot get enough oxygen to readily burn. Also, most fire departments are so rapid in their response to fire alarms, and so effective in the treatment of fires, that many times fires are put out long before very much of a collection is put at risk. In recent years, natural disasters such as earthquakes and the hazards they bring with them, such as flooding from broken pipes, have caused more damage to libraries than fires.

With most fires, smoke causes more damage to the collections than the fire it-self. A small fire in one area of the library can send smoke throughout the entire collection. Paper is very absorbent and will readily trap the smell of smoke in its pages, while the smoke can leave a thick, dark, often oily film on the covers of the books that can be hard to remove. If a fire breaks out in your library, be prepared to have to rebind many hundreds of books both because of the fire damage and because of the smoke damage. Work with your fire department to let them know that the smoke needs to be cleared from the building as rapidly as possible. Most fire departments do this as standard practice these days. They know that smoke is often more damaging than the fire itself, so they are experienced in ventilating the building as soon as possible.

The heat from the fire can greatly damage paper, making it become brittle and weak. There is nothing that can be done to strengthen the paper. But there are some options for coping with the smoke smells in the paper. Standing the books on a table and fanning them open with a fan blowing over them for several days will help. It is also possible to treat the smell with ozone. This is effective, but it is also damaging to the paper. Ozone is O3 that is extremely reactive. Ozone molecules readily want to shed one of the oxygen atoms to become O2. This aggressive oxidation process is what eliminates the odor, but the ozone will also attack the paper molecules causing it to breakdown. Therefore, if your library plans to permanently keep the books in its collections, it is probably best not to use ozone treatment because the long-term effect of the cure for the odor may be more damaging than the odors themselves. Several of the disaster-recovery firms offer ozone treatment for odors, and it is important that you make an informed decision about the offered treatment.

The largest risk to books and papers is water. Again, water is a primary or sec-ondary risk in almost all major disasters from fire to earthquakes. Therefore, most disaster-recovery firms are set up to rapidly deal with water-damaged collections. The two primary concerns for paper in water damage is blocking and mold. Blocking is when glossy or coated papers literally adhere together so that the pages become one block of paper. Coated paper will begin to block as soon as the paper starts to dry. If blocking begins there is nothing that can be done to reverse the process. The only treatment is to get the book frozen quickly until it can be freeze-dried or until the pages can be separated and air-dried.

Mold is a bigger risk. Mold spores are in the air all of the time, and a mold outbreak will occur any time the conditions are right for the mold spores to germinate. There are many different kinds of molds, but most common "house-hold" molds take about forty-eight hours to germinate and reproduce. Nearly all of the molds found in libraries are not dangerous to humans—though many people have allergies to them. However, they are dirty, smell bad, and are naturally repulsive. If conditions are favorable, a mold outbreak can spread very rapidly. Often people will call me and say things such as, "I checked it last night and things were fine, and this morning when I got to work the entire place was covered with fuzzy mold."

Most molds can only grow when the temperature is above seventy degrees Fahrenheit, with 60 to 70 percent relative humidity. These figures can be tricky, because we are talking about the conditions of a very small space. Think of your shower. Why does mildew (which is mold) want to grow on the shower walls but not on the bathroom walls? The answer is that the shower walls regularly get wet and have a high enough relative humidity and temperature to support mold growth, where the bathroom walls—six inches away—do not have the same conditions. Therefore, if a library book gets wet, it can have a high enough relative humidity for mold to grow on the book, even though the air in the library may be very dry. Therefore, in a water-related disaster, it is important to lower the temperature below seventy degrees and to get the air circulating in the disaster area. Large fans can be rented from most equipment rental places. Keep these fans circulating the air night and day. Also, it is important to keep the lights on. Ultraviolet lights kill most molds, and all overhead lights produce some ultraviolet light.

Another concern for wet books is leather. Leather—especially damaged, red-rotted leather—does not react well to water. It is important to get this material frozen or air-dried as quickly as possible. Unless the leather-bound volume is a library treasure or part of a special collection, it is usually best to concentrate efforts on preserving the text of the volume and rebind the book later.

Wet books and paper can absorb a *great* deal of water. The effect is extremely heavy books that swell with the water, often splitting their bindings and sometime wedging themselves so tightly on the shelves they are difficult to remove. It is important not to move these heavy, weakened materials any more than necessary. If conditions require it, remove the materials to a clean staging area where they can be processed for drying, but otherwise try to minimize the amount of stress put on wet materials caused by excessive shifting.

Film-Based Materials

Most libraries have some film-based materials like microfilm or microfiche. Some libraries have large movie or video collections. All film-based materials are made of a plastic support covered with a gelatin layer in which the image is produced or the recording components are held. Gelatin is a water-soluble adhesive that will begin to separate from the film carrier when exposed to water. Generally this takes forty-eight to seventy-two hours. If only a few films get wet, they can be unrolled and air-dried, but generally it is easier and more economic to have the films reproduced. Many commercially produced films can easily be replaced (often with a digital version). If a film was produced by the library, or if no other copies can be easily obtained, then it is important to keep the water-damaged film wet and ship it to a vendor that can produce a new copy of the film.

Because films have gelatin, it is important to carefully check the films in your collections to make sure they did not get wet. Even a little water on a film can cause the films to block together—permanently ruining them. Also, because of the gelatin, film-based materials will readily support mold growth. Therefore it is important to keep the temperature and relative humidity low following a disaster. This may mean opening the film cabinet drawers to allow adequate air circulation.

Because film-based materials are regularly stored in cabinets, they often escape many of the effects of a disaster that books experience sitting on open shelving. The cabinets are effective at protecting against smoke, debris, and water. However, what the cabinets do not protect against is heat. Heat can be extremely damaging to film-based materials. The heat can dry out the film and make it brittle; it can shrink and warp the plastic and can cause the film to melt together and burn.

One final word about film-based collections: All film materials are relatively new technology compared to paper, and the medium has undergone a lot of changes over the decades. This means it is complicated stuff and expensive to treat in the event of a disaster. The good news is that technology has largely made film an obsolete storage medium as this information is now mostly stored digitally. Therefore, you need to determine if you can replace the information with a digital copy and, if you can, whether that will be less expensive than trying to salvage the existing film.

Computers

Computers are the most important information tools in libraries. They are used not only by patrons for accessing information but also by nearly every staff member in his or her daily work of processing materials for the collections. Therefore, no disaster plan is complete without addressing computers. Our society has become so reliant on computer technology that most libraries are probably covered by a computer-recovery contract or agreement established by the parent organization such as the college, the city, the county, or the state.

These agreements are generally established to ensure large government agencies will be able to keep important servers and databases up and functioning. However, sometimes the contracts also cover desktop machines. It is important to find out what agreements are in place and how they apply to your library. As said earlier, these IT disaster plans are often created by professionals outside of the library, and they do not always communicate the details of the plan to library staff, so it is important to be proactive and know, *before* a disaster strikes, what services are available.

Computers and servers are very sensitive to fire-related disasters. Not only do the fire and heat cause problems, but the smoke presents a serious hazard as well. The smoke from fires in modern buildings will be full of chlorine and sulfur ions that will mix with the moisture in the air to form hydrochloric and sulfuric acids that will quickly destroy the delicate circuitry inside the computers and monitors. This can happen in less than twenty-four hours. Many fire departments are aware of this hazard and take steps to prevent it by covering computers with plastic and ventilating the building. Most disaster-recovery firms also have a great deal of experience dealing with computer-related materials and can help your library recover from a fire- or water-based disaster if your computers and servers are not already covered by a larger computer-based recovery contract. It is important to meet with your insurance company and come to an agreement about what they are willing to do for your library in terms of recovering or replacing computer equipment.

Recovery and Replacement Costs

It is extremely important for your library and insurance agency to come to an understanding about what it will cost to recover from a major disaster. As mentioned before, most disasters involve water—often resulting in a large amount of library binding. This is a relatively inexpensive recovery cost, but when discussing thousands of volumes the cost can be significant. Other books will have to be replaced. It is important for the library to understand what percentage of the replacement cost the insurance will pay.

On large disasters, it is almost always less expensive, in the long run, to hire the services of a reputable disaster-recovery firm. Responding quickly to a disaster by hiring a good recovery firm will result in a high percentage of recovered books and computers, less damage to the building, and a quicker return to normal operations. Many insurance companies understand this. Make sure yours does.

When replacing books and computers the question that often comes up is, do you replace like for like, or do you replace cost for cost? For example, your library has a fire in which a dozen five-year-old computers are lost. Does the insurance pay to replace them with similar computers that are out of date and very inexpensive? This will be replacing exactly what was lost and will save the insurance company thousands of dollars. Or do they replace them with new computers? Books are the same way. A library book that was destroyed in a fire may cost twenty-five dollars to buy it again, but it will cost a library double or triple that cost to process it and return it to the shelf. What part of that cost is covered by the insurance policy? Your insurance company has probably already thought about these questions. You need to know what their policies are and work out an agreement that is acceptable for both your library and the insurance company. It might mean checking with other insurance companies to find a policy that better meets the needs of your library. These are important questions that need to be settled with your insurance company *before* a disaster strikes.

Understanding the disaster threats that are most likely to strike your library, and the recovery options available, will help the library be prepared to deal with disasters when they occur. Disasters, by their very nature, are unpredictable, dynamic events. It is impossible to have a plan developed to exactly deal with every aspect of every disaster. However, the plan can provide general guidelines for getting the patrons and the staff out of the library, notifying the proper authorities, and getting the disaster team in place so they can begin to cope with the situation based on their expertise, experience, and understanding of the resources available.

All libraries will face some kind of a disaster sometime—whether large or small. Learning from these experiences will help further prepare your library to cope with the next disaster when it comes along. Also, take advantage of library disaster networks that might exist in your state or region. Often these organizations provide opportunities for training and for sharing of war stories. This is an important activity. Take advantage of opportunities to learn from the successes and mistakes of other libraries so you can apply these practical experiences to any future disaster situations faced by your own library. Invariably, you will leave a conference or workshop about disaster planning having picked up some practical information that you would not have thought of before.

Finally, it is important for the library staff to experience what it is like to deal with wet volumes. One of the examples I usually give at most disaster-training workshops I provide is to start the workshop by holding up a large reference volume printed on newsprint type of paper with over a thousand pages. These are not as common as they once were when libraries had lots of paper index volumes, but a large phone book will work too. I show this book to people and then drop it into a five-gallon bucket of water. Near the end of the workshop I pull the book out and show the group how much water it has absorbed. These large books will often absorb two or more gallons of water. I let the class feel the weight of the book. I let them experience how unwieldy it is. I open the cover and show them how things like library identification stamps or other inks have moved into the pages as the water wicks through the book. I show how bookplates might have floated off, how the cover is delaminated, or other problems that one might not anticipate without actually seeing a thoroughly wetted book up close. This is a simple but dramatic example from which a great deal can be learned.

In like manner, it is also a good idea to wet other kinds of materials to see how they behave under such conditions. Allow some microformatted materials to soak in water for a few days prior to the workshop to show how the layers begin to separate. Get a book with glossy paper wet and observe how blocking occurs. These are valuable experiences that will be of great benefit in dealing with future disasters and could result in saving the library tens of thousands of dollars.

Recovery Efforts

As mentioned earlier, it is usually best to secure the services of a professional recovery company when dealing with major disasters, but every library finds itself faced with small disasters on a fairly regular basis. Small leaks, patrons returning wet books, or staff accidents can all result in wet books. Therefore, it is important to say a few words about how to effectively air-dry a book.

Lay blotter paper or clean newsprint on the tables or floor where the wet materials will be placed. Have enough fans blowing over the materials to keep the air circulating around all of the wet items so the materials will dry and mold will not grow. Keep the lights on at all times, and the temperature low (below seventy degrees F) to reduce the chance of mold growth. Stand the bound volumes upright on their top or bottom edge, and open the covers to about a ninety-degree angle. Fan the pages out as much as possible to allow for maximum airflow (see figure 10.1). If a volume will not stand up, lay it on its side and interleave the pages of the text block with paper towels.

Place the volumes far enough apart to allow air to flow around and through each volume. Drying time will depend on the amount of wetness, the size of the volume, and the type of paper. Check on the volumes often, and rotate the wet volumes closer to the fans and the drier ones farther away. Rotate standing volumes from their top to bottom edges every few hours as they are drying so the paper dries evenly. Separate the pages by refanning them as they dry. This will help the volume dry evenly and will help keep the pages from sticking together. *Watch closely for glossy papers!* Glossy papers often stick together if they

Figure 10.1 Example of how wet books are placed on a table for air-drying

get wet. If they dry stuck together, they can't be separated. Take time during the drying process to turn every glossy page in the book to make sure they do not stick together. This will usually need to be done a couple of times if a volume with glossy paper is completely wet.

As the volumes dry, sometimes the paper and boards will begin to cockle and warp. Many water-damaged books will have to be rebound, but it is important for the paper to be pressed flat before it is sent for binding. When the paper is clearly dry, but still cool to the touch, place the volume under weight to help the paper relax and flatten out again. Multiple volumes can be stacked on top of one another as long as even pressure can be maintained.

The most important aspect of disaster planning and recovery efforts is common sense. Do not get bogged down in minutia. Disasters, by their very nature, are unpredictable and dynamic. A good plan will quickly direct the staff and patrons on how to effectively cope with the immediate effects of a disaster situation. From there it is simply a matter of using common sense and good judgment on how best to proceed. By understanding the main concerns for the safety of the staff, the patrons, and the collections, good decisions can be made to preserve as many lives and materials as possible in any situation that presents itself.

Chapter 11

Digital Preservation

Preservation impacts every department in a library, but in larger libraries preservation's traditional activities are usually handled by a standalone department, or by a technical services unit in smaller libraries. Digital preservation does not follow that model. Proof of this can be seen in the course catalogs of most library schools where courses in digital preservation are taught as part of collection development, systems administration, cataloging, archives, preservation, and so forth.

Part of the reason digital preservation is discussed in so many courses is because electronic information is so ubiquitous, and part of it is because electronic information introduces a number of technical challenges that are unique to this medium. In the twenty-first century, it is important to think about electronic information as information, and not as a "type" of information. When approached this way, then the courses in library school make more sense. In the past, all information was paper based, so courses were not taught about cataloging paper-based collections. The course was just called cataloging because we did not really need to qualify what kind of medium the information was stored on. Later, we started to specify cataloging for special collections as opposed to general collections. Later still we started to specify various storage mediums. Cataloging electronic information is just an extension of the same activity except that it is becoming the largest format used. Library schools started to specify specific courses on electronic information when it was a smaller part of our library collections. Now it is the majority of our collections, and it is time to stop thinking about electronic information as a subset when making preservation plans.

Digital preservation is often compared to a three-legged stool with management, content, and technology making up the three legs. This is true, but it is also true for paper-based collections. We have to acquire and build electronic collections (collection development), manage the information (technical services), and cope with the infrastructure required to house and make the information available (facilities management). The point is, there is more that is familiar to us about electronic collections than there is that is different. Librarians are experts at acquiring, organizing, and making information available. Electronic information is a new dynamic format, but the general processes and strategies are largely the same. This is also true for digital preservation. The overall strategies for what to consider when preserving a digital collection are the same. You have to assess the collection, identify the preservation risks, and create strategies for proactively managing the data you need to preserve. That is why this chapter is presented at the end of the book rather than at the beginning. The reader will find many of the strategies and thought processes discussed in previous chapters are very relevant for digital preservation. But that said, there are some very important key differences, and we will address them.

Libraries have always acquired, housed, and preserved collections. In the past these were physical items stored in the library. Libraries had an obligation to preserve their collections because they owned them. It was part of their stewardship to the community they served rather than some moral or philosophical commitment to the greater good of humanity.

We have discussed in this book that preservation should always be a team effort with goals being achieved through consensus and synergistic efforts. But in the end, when the rubber meets the road, traditional preservation services involves work that is quantifiable, performed by trained individuals in a department, with an assigned budget for this work. The digital age changed this. Digital preservation is an archives issue, a technical services issue, and IT issue, and a collection-development issue. A library that has no traditional preservation could easily have a strong digital-preservation program and not even think of it as such.

Digital preservation must answer questions such as follows:

- How do we ensure continued access to electronic subscriptions?
- Who is responsible for preserving electronic books we purchase or lease?
- How do we preserve digital information created by our institution?

Libraries have always had a natural tension between technical services and public services. They both share the same big goals and ideals but have differing objectives that sometimes compete against each other. Digital preservation moves this tension outside of the library walls to struggles between the library and the parent organization's information technology department. Or to an even larger stage such as the library profession versus publishers, or international copyright law.

The good news is that we are no longer rowing against the tide. We have crossed the digital Rubicon and are firmly in the digital age. Information providers sell or lease their information to libraries in a digital format, and they are highly motivated to make certain they preserve the content they offer. The onus for preservation has, in many cases, shifted from the library that used to buy and own its information to the publisher or aggregator who supplies the electronic information to the library. Even in cases when libraries do buy electronic information, they do not own the rights to reformat, or copy, or migrate it to a newer technology. The publisher owns those rights and is motivated to move the information forward to remain competitive.

This is the big difference for much of the information a library acquires today. In the past, if a library did not preserve its information it would lose it. It could take decades for this to happen sometimes, but if the library did not take action no one else would feel obligated to preserve the information. Now, much of the information acquired by the library will be preserved, or not preserved, despite any efforts made by the library. We are like a flea on an elephant's back. We are pretty much stuck with going for a ride. But again, this is a ride we are used to as librarians. We have always been subject to the whims of publishers and have developed our collection policies accordingly. In the past a library had to buy a book soon after it was published because it was often not able to get a copy later. In recent years with print-on-demand technology and electronic information this has changed. Libraries are able to adjust their collection-development policies to allow them to wait to purchase titles until after a user has requested it. Libraries adjusted their acquisition policies because of changes in the publishing industry, not because they demanded the publishers to change.

The two big differences between paper-based collections and electronic information are as follows:

- In the past if a library missed getting a book it was one book, and they could interlibrary loan a copy. Now, if a publisher drops an entire series of e-journals they are gone for everyone.
- The changes in technology exacerbate the problem as publishers have to decide what information to migrate forward to a new delivery platform on a regular basis.

History has demonstrated that popular information will move forward from one format to the next. For example, the Bible has always been one of the first things made available in a new information technology, be that printing, audiobooks, e-books, or the web. But what about less popular works such as B movies or independent films from the past? What happens to the works by musical groups with a small fan base, or the books that sell poorly or that are now self-published (which is the vast majority of books)? Even more challenging, how do we preserve very dynamic information such as web pages—especially political or controversial web pages? These are new and dynamic problems and present preservation dilemmas we never faced before.

When I was working with Eastern European state libraries to help them assess their collections and establish preservation plans, we saw many books on the libraries' shelves that the dictatorial governments had banned and even ordered destroyed. Most of these items were kept as a result of benign neglect. They were added to the library as part of their normal workflow and forgotten about. Seventy years later the desire to have them destroyed was gone, and everyone was glad that no one had taken the proactive effort to follow the government mandate to destroy these books. In the digital age benign neglect will result in information being lost, not preserved. We have to be much more proactive about our preservation efforts than ever before.

Over the years preservation of information has always been a key mission for libraries, but while it is important, it is rarely viewed as an urgent priority. However, digital preservation is both important and urgent! This problem is further compounded by the tremendous volume of information we have to preserve. The digital age has dramatically lowered (or all but removed) the entrance barrier to publishing or producing a book, magazine, movie, or music album. Thus the volume of information that is available is growing at an even larger exponential rate than it has been in recent decades. This creates challenges for all aspects of librarianship such as collection development, cataloging (metadata), and preservation.

Finally, a unique challenge we face with digital preservation is that publishers and information providers go to great lengths to keep their products from being pirated. As a result, the sophisticated encryption algorithms present difficult challenges to preserving electronic information and migrating it forward, forcing the responsibility back to the publisher. Again, it is easy to feel like a flea on the elephant's back. But things are not as dire as they may appear at first blush. While one flea has little effect on an elephant, thousands and thousands of them can make an elephant take action. Electronic information brings a lot of unique and difficult preservation challenges, but one advantage it offers is that it allows cooperative efforts and division of duties that make this large task manageable.

Digital preservation involves answering questions about their collections that librarians have always had to address, but the scale and context for these questions are a little different. Libraries need to answer the following questions about their digital collections at both the local and national levels:

- Just because it can be preserved, should it be preserved?
- What responsibility does my organization have for preserving this information?
- What steps must be taken to preserve this information (e.g., metadata, storage space, and delivery platforms)?

As professionals, we need to take an active role in the larger digital-preservation discussions taking place. Most libraries will only face practical digital-preservation issues as they relate to their local archives and special collections. We will discuss this more below. But librarians should lend their voices, time, and energy to the larger issues at their state, regional, and national library organizations, and through cooperative purchasing groups. The digital age makes it easier than ever for libraries to work together cooperatively for important causes. The downside is that it is easy to become complacent and tell ourselves that others will take care of the problem, that others will advocate for the preservation of the information we are using. It is like the proverb that says show me a boat owned by two men and I will show you a leaky boat. When something becomes everyone's responsibility it too often becomes no one's responsibility. We have to guard against this complacency.

But even if we want to be proactive it can be challenging at times. Remember the three-legged stool analogy. It is human nature to become territorial, and if a librarian works in collection development and wants to advocate for preserving a digital collection, he or she has to be careful about not stepping on the toes of the library staff members who are in charge of, say, electronic subscriptions, cataloging/metadata creation, or information technology. As stated in the first chapter of this book, preservation in the twenty-first century is largely about cooperation, and digital preservation, both at the local and national level, is a perfect example of this. Digital preservation requires our best cooperative efforts, careful planning, and taking a long-term view. By working together, with each library staff member doing his or her relevant part, progress can be made and goals achieved. But these efforts have to become proceduralized because electronic information that is safe today may be at great risk in the very near future. With paper-based collections, if a book gets library bound or a conservation treatment, it is preserved for centuries to come. A policy to preserve a digital collection that is robust and thorough today may become invalid in the near future when technology changes.

We will now look at some specifics to consider with digitization, metadata creation, and migration. Almost all libraries have some treasures they want to digitize. We will address general concepts and strategies because digitization and digital preservation are so dynamic that any details or practices other than general guidelines will be out of date in a short time. Furthermore, there are lots of resources and training opportunities available from places like the Library of Congress, the National Archives, the American Library Association, and regional preservation centers. As a general rule it is best to get training or begin to further your preservation learning when you have a specific project in hand.

Digitization

There are two ways of creating electronic information. Either it is born digital, meaning it was created as an electronic file and only has to be preserved in that format, or an analog original is reformatted into a digital version. This can be paper, film, or analog sound recordings. Just because we use electronic equipment to deliver the information (such as a movie projector or a tape recorder) does not mean the information is digitally stored. There are pros and cons to having analog information, and debates continue about whether an analog copy should be maintained. Each situation is unique, but it is important to understand the arguments and the issues. One of the strongest arguments for keeping an analog copy is that in the event of a huge disaster, where electrical power is lost, many analog forms of information can still be used. It may be difficult to read a microfilm without a modern reader, but it can be done with a light source and simple magnification.

The important thing to remember with any digitization project is that creating the digital file is only part of the project. Creating metadata and making decisions about how to present and store the digital information can be very involved. And how the information will be presented needs to be taken into consideration prior to beginning the digitization.

As a general rule, it is a good idea to create the highest quality possible of a digital copy. You can always make lower-resolution copies from the high-resolution master, but you cannot go the other way. Over the years best practices have changed regarding how high the resolution should be for master files. So check to see what the current best practices are at the time you are ready to start a project.

As with reformatting practices for microfilm, when creating a digital format you generally want a master file from which use files are created. The master file should be in an open source or standard format like TIFF files for images, but this too is dynamic. As certain file formats become ubiquitous they become a sort of default standard just because of their sheer volume such as JPEG or PDF files. The idea is to keep the master file in a noncompressed, or nonloss compressed, format that is stable and will be around long into the future. Creating files in a proprietary format could prove problematic if that company goes out of business. We have seen this several times in popular media formats such as

VHS versus Beta videos, competing compact disc formats, and Blu-ray versus HD DVD. Having noncompressed, open-source files greatly increases the ease in migrating the master files forward to new technology (see below).

Digitization is a labor-intensive process, and care needs to be taken to make sure the master files are as complete and error free as possible. Most shortcuts taken in the digitization process are usually paid for later when trying to create use copies, or migrating the data forward. Again, the general premise is that you can easily create a lesser-quality derivative copy, but you cannot improve on the original file produced during the reformatting effort, and if you miss images, or the created copies are not useable, it takes real effort to go back, find the missing information, and update the master file. In short, the digitization part of the project is not the time to be sloppy and to make a lot of compromises. Do whatever is possible to create the best quality digital file possible.

Metadata

Creation of good metadata for digital files is crucial. It is more important than cataloging is to paper-based collections, and every librarian understands how important cataloging is. Digital information can grow and expand so quickly that without good metadata controls the files soon become unmanageable.

Metadata, which is data about data, provides the needed information to manage the files, know what information they contain, and how the files were created. Metadata is also important for helping you preserve and migrate your digital files.

There are, basically, three categories of metadata for library information:

Descriptive: This metadata is used to identify what the files contain. It is about the information in the files. It describes the information. Descriptive meta-data is similar to the information we gather while cataloging traditional library collections such as title and author information, keywords, search terms, and physical attributes. This is the information needed to allow users to find items when they do a web search.

Structural: This metadata is used to navigate within the file or collection and to present the information to the user. It provides details about the organization of the content or items in the collections. When using an e-book the structural metadata is what allows you to go to a specific chapter or page number in the book. It is how links from pictures or maps to a specific part of the text are created.

Administrative: This metadata is used to manage the digital collection, during both immediate and long-term use. Preservation metadata is administrative in nature. This data gives information about how the files were created, when it was created, usage limitations, and file types. It is also used to establish schedules for when and how to migrate the information forward complete with data (like checksums) for determining if the files were copied or migrated completely.

In the late 1990s, when digitization projects were new, most of the metadata work was done by preservation experts, and in larger preservation operations this is often still the case, but the majority of libraries now have metadata experts on staff who deal with metadata for the electronic information they acquire for their collections. They do not always have skill sets in all three areas of metadata, but learning the specifics for, say, preservation metadata is usually a simple matter for them if they are already immersed in working with metadata on a daily basis. Make sure you find out what expertise exists in your library, and do not reinvent the wheel.

Storage and Migration

If good digitization and thorough, consistent metadata practices were followed, then the storage and migration part of digital preservation becomes much easier. This area of the process is usually controlled by the IT department and, as a result, can fall prey to the traditional bane of preservation, meaning it is viewed as important but not urgent. Thus, the risk of loss due to neglect is a real issue. It is, therefore, important to incorporate digital storage and migration into the regular IT work stream as much as possible. If the storage and migration of digital collections is outside of IT's normal procedures, or requires a lot of extra effort, it greatly increases the odds that it will not happen.

Migration is the process of moving digital information from one distribution package or software to a new one. An example most of us deal with on a regular basis is migrating word-processing or spreadsheet files from an older version of the software to a newer version. You will often see a popup window asking if you want to convert the file, and then warning that once converted it will not be able to be opened with an older version of the software. Sometimes we have to convert an older file that was created on a different operation system or into a different company's word-processing software. The software companies provide conversion tools that makes this migration possible, but the older the file is, or the more generations it is behind the current software, the harder it is to convert, and often high-level formatting, or embedded images or tables, will become corrupted. This same principle applies to migrating digital information. This is why it is important to pick file formats for the preservation master files that are standard and have been around, and are likely to continue to be around into the future. It is also why the metadata is so important. It helps ensure the people in the future migrating the data know all they need to know to enable them to convert the files over to the new format.

Note that moving files forward from one storage medium to the next is not migration. Migration is the process of converting files. This is needed when the presentation software changes. Moving files forward and keeping them alive is an easier process than migration. Moving files to a new server, or to a cloud storage system, can be an automated process. Migration requires an active decision, and the converted files need to be checked carefully to make sure the conversion was complete and accurate. The trouble is that just like the word-processing example given earlier we often do not realize we need to migrate a file forward until we try to open it in the new software package and discover there is a problem. The problem is usually discovered by the collection-development staff or the public service staff who are made aware of the problem by patrons, but after the problem is discovered the migration or conversion usually goes back to being an IT problem. The result is that having a proactive migration policy for their various digital collections can be challenging to libraries, but there are good strategies out there, and just like with disaster planning, you can learn from the lessons of others by attending sessions on migration at conferences, and by reading published papers on the topic.

Digital preservation is a huge, dynamic challenge, and the sad reality is that a lot of information created during the first part of the twenty-first century will be lost to future generations. This has always been the case with emerging technology. Not all manuscript documents got converted to printed books. Not all film-based movies have been converted to video or digital formats. The popular works get converted. The classics get moved forward. But information will be lost. As a society, and as a library profession, we can work to minimize the loss, but loss will occur. With a concerted, proactive approach in your library you can minimize the loss of the treasures only your institution holds. Focus on what you can control, and use what resources, time, and energy you have left to contribute to the greater cause.

Conclusion

The most important component of an effective library preservation program is common sense. Sound preservation planning involves critically evaluating the collections and practices of the library to determine what should be changed to help preserve the collections and increase access to information. After an overall preservation plan is in place, a library can use this contextual understanding to develop specific preservation strategies. These strategies can then guide the library in seeking the specific preservation training or expertise needed to further its preservation and collection-development goals. However, every step of the process must be guided by practical leadership with the long-term needs of the library in mind. It must also be remembered—especially in the twenty-first century—that libraries, and the information they make available to their patrons, are *very* dynamic. Therefore, the preservation plans have to be dynamic too and need to be reviewed on a regular basis to ensure that the plan remains valid.

When preservation efforts are firmly grounded on the foundation of the library's overall collection-development policy, then administrators can be confident that preservation efforts are worth the investment of staff time and other resources. Staff members who receive preservation training will be more likely to accept changes in their current procedures and apply what they have learned because they will understand preservation efforts in the context of the library's overall goals.

Preservation impacts every aspect of librarianship. Purchasing decisions, processing procedures, shelving practices, and staff and user training all impact the life expectancy of the materials purchased for the library. This manual has, in each of its chapters, looked at specific preservation activities, but in conclusion it is important to be reminded again that to be most effective, preservation activities must be viewed at a macro, library-wide level. Preservation is a constant struggle to balance resources, library-wide policies and strategies, patron needs, and the long-term plans for the collections. This is why preservation is a constant process of assessment and evaluation. There are never enough resources to meet all of the preservation needs of a library. Therefore, preservation must optimize the use of the resources available to have the largest impact possible. This has been the overriding premise of this manual, and understanding this principle will enable a library to effectively preserve its collections in the most efficient manner possible.

Finally, do not become frustrated by being unable to accomplish all of the preservation efforts your library needs. Take a long-term approach. Every little bit helps, and the benefits cumulatively add up over time. Within just a few years you will be surprised by the positive impact your preservation efforts are making.

Appendix

Useful Websites and Vendors

Websites

American Library Association, Association for Library Collections and Technical Services, Preservation and Reformatting Section, http://www.ala.org/alcts/mgrps/pars

Conservation OnLine (CoOL), http://cool.conservation-us.org

Dartmouth College Library's Preservation Services' "Simple Book Repair Manual," https://www.dartmouth.edu/~library/preservation/repair/index.html

Library of Congress preservation website, https://www.loc.gov/preservation

LYRASIS Library Services, http://www.lyrasis.org

National Archives preservation website, https://www.archives.gov/preservation

Northeast Document Conservation Center (NEDCC), https://www.nedcc.org

Regional Alliance for Preservation, http://www.rap-arcc.org

Vendors

Archival Products
PO Box 1413
Des Moines, IA 50305-1413
800-526-5640
Fax: 888-220-2397
custserv@archival.com
http://www.archival.com

Conservation Resources, International
5532 Port Royal Road
Springfield, VA 22151
800-634-6932
Fax: 703-321-0629
sales@conservationresources.com
http://www.conservationresources.com

Gaylord Brothers
PO Box 4901
Syracuse, NY 13221-4901
800-448-6160
Fax: 800-272-3412
customerservice@gaylord.com
http://www.gaylord.com

Hollinger Metal Edge
9401 Northeast Drive
Fredericksburg, VA 22408
800-634-0491
info@hollingermetaledge.com
http://www.hollingermetaledge.com

Talas
330 Morgan Avenue
Brooklyn, NY 11211
212-219-0770
http://www.talasonline.com

University Products
517 Main Street
Holyoke, MA 01040
800-628-1912
Fax: 800-532-9281
info@universityproducts.com
http://www.universityproducts.com

Glossary

acidic paper. Beginning in about 1850, papermakers began using wood fiber to produce their paper. Wood fiber makes strong, consistent paper, but it requires harsh chemicals to break the wood down into fibers suitable to produce paper. As a result, residual chemicals remain in the paper after it is produced. Until the 1980s, most paper production in the world involved harsh acids that were left in the paper causing it to become weak and brittle over time. Most paper produced in the United States and in Western Europe is now alkaline in nature and will last for several hundred years.

analog. *Analog* is a term that has quite different meanings based on the context of how it is being used, whether discussing storage medium, radio signals, or sound production. For libraries, analog refers to nondigital information sources such as paper, film-based media, or sound recordings. There are debates about the need to preserve an analog version of information for long-term preservation.

brittle paper. Acidic paper begins to break down by turning yellow or brown, as the acids in the paper break down the fibers. The result of acid degradation makes the paper brittle and weak. Paper can become so brittle that it will literally crumble to bits in your hands. Both heat and moisture act as catalysts in paper to increase the acidic degradation of paper.

collection condition survey. A statistical method of analyzing the condition of the materials housed in a library's collection. The questions asked as part of the survey and the size of the sample are dependent on the informational needs of the library. Generally, more than one survey is needed to gather all the information necessary to produce an effective preservation plan for a library. Conducting a statistically valid survey is not difficult, but it does require care to ensure the data gathered are valid and meaningful to the library's planning efforts.

crash or super. The cloth or other material placed on the spine of a text block of hardcover books designed both to consolidate the text block and to secure the case binding to the text block.

digital preservation. The process of preserving information that comes to the library in an electronic format, or is reformatted by the library to create a digital copy. Digital preservation is dynamic and introduces new challenges, and involves several departments in the library. Digital preservation is the biggest preservation issue facing libraries today.

digitization. A reformatting process where images, printed materials, or other analog publications are scanned to create a digital copy of the information. This is often done for access purposes so that information can be shared on the web or through online platforms provided by the library.

endsheets. The first and last pages of a text block on a hardcover volume. They are glued to the inside of the case binding to securely hold the text block into the case. These are called pastedowns. The free sheet remaining is called a flyleaf. Generally, the endsheets are made of thicker, stronger paper to provide extra support.

flat back. This is a binding method used by most library binders. In flat-back binding the text block is not rounded and backed, so it has no shoulders and no curved spine. The cover hinge is generally wider than on a rounded and backed book. Most binders offer flat-back bindings on their economy products. Some binders offer only this binding style on all of their products. Some leaf-attachment methods (such as polyurethane reactive [PUR] and other perfect bindings) cannot be rounded and backed, so a flat-back binding is the only option.

HVAC system. Stands for heating, ventilation, and air-conditioning system. It is important for a library to understand the specifications for its HVAC system and to work closely with facilities people to optimize the HVAC systems operation proficiency so that the library has the best environmental conditions possible for its collections.

inner margin. This is the distance from the edge of the text in a bound volume to the inside gutter of the book. Inner margin is an important consideration when making binding decisions. If text runs through the gutter of a book, it may be lost if the book has to be rebound.

metadata. Metadata is data about data. There are several different kinds of metadata used to describe, organize, and manage electronic information. This includes preservation metadata needed to preserve the electronic information. Metadata serves the same purpose for electronic information as cataloging does for printed collections.

preservation plan. Simply stated, this is a library's strategy for addressing the preservation needs of its collections. An effective preservation plan includes identifying what preservation needs exist, what resources are available to commit toward preservation, and what long-term plans are in place for meeting the needs unable to be addressed by current resources. It is impossible to have a good preservation plan without careful and thorough assessment including a collection condition survey.

publisher binding. A binding placed on a volume by the publisher. Generally, these bindings are produced as quickly and as inexpensively as possible, and do not provide a great deal of strength and support to the book. Some publishers provide stronger bindings than others. Understanding how publisher bindings—especially publisher paper bindings—hold up to use in a library has important implications for preservation planning.

PUR adhesive. PUR stands for polyurethane reactive adhesive. It is a hot-melt adhesive used in bookbinding as a leaf-attachment method. Unlike other perfect-binding methods, PUR adhesive is extremely strong and flexible and meets or exceeds the requirements specified in the LBI/NISO/ANSI library binding standard.

rounding and backing. This is the process of shaping a text block so that it has its traditional look of a rounded back with flared shoulders. Traditionally, rounding and backing was made necessary because the thickness of the thread used to sew the text block together caused the spine to swell. The rounded shape of the spine and the flared shoulders compensated for this swell. Whether or not rounding and backing is needed in library binding has been a hotly debated issue.

saddle stitch. When a publication is made up of one signature that is stapled through the fold it is called saddle stitched. Saddle stitching is common in pamphlets and many magazines such as *Time*, *Sports Illustrated*, and *People*. Saddle-sewn journals can be bound by a library binder without having to chop off the spine.

shelf-preparation activities. Those procedures routinely conducted on materials purchased for the library prior to their being shelved in the collection. For example, spine labeling, paperback stiffening, prebinding, dust-jacket protectors, and book training are all considered shelf-preparation activities.

statistically valid. Collection condition surveys and other library assessment tools often rely on statistical procedures for gathering and analyzing data. Statistically based surveys must be conducted under strict operational procedures to ensure that the data are statistically valid—meaning they can be used to accurately predict characteristics of the population from which the sample was taken.

temperature and relative humidity. These are the primary measures for determining the environmental conditions of a library. It is important to control the temperature and relative humidity, because both can act as catalysts to accelerate the acid degradation of paper and other library materials. The goal for all libraries and museums is to try, as much as possible, to maintain a constant temperature and relative humidity with a temperature of about seventy degrees Fahrenheit with about 40 percent relative humidity.

text block. The pages of a bound volume make up the text block. There are many ways of producing a text block ranging from sewing signatures together to make the text block and to gluing individual sheets together to make up the text of the volume. How a text block was prepared by the publisher impacts how a library binder can rebind the volume.

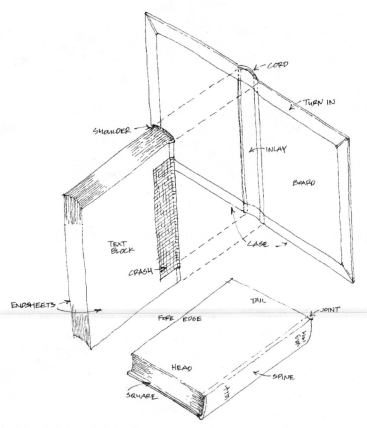

Figure G.1 Parts of a book

Bibliography

Baird, Brian J. "Case Binding with Flexible Bonnet: A Specification for General Library Collections." *New Library Scene* 13 (October 1994): 8–10.

———. "Commercial Binding as a Preservation Treatment." *New Library Scene* 14 (October 1995): 5–6, 8, 22.

———. "Goals and Objectives of Collections Conservation." *Restaurator* 13 (1992): 149–61.

———. *Library Collection Assessment through Statistical Sampling.* Lanham, MD: Scarecrow, 2004.

———. "A Look at Microenvironments for Books." *New Library Scene* 13 (April 1994): 8–12.

———. "Paperbacks vs. Hardbacks: Answers from the University of Kansas Libraries' Condition Survey." *Abbey Newsletter* 20, no. 6 (December 15, 1996): 93–95. http://palimpsest.stanford.edu.

———. "Pioneering the Use of Polyurethane Adhesive in Library Binding." *Serials Librarian* 61, no. 2 (Spring 2011): 275–82.

———. *Preservation Strategies for Small Academic and Public Libraries.* Lanham, MD: Scarecrow, 2003.

———. *Preserving Your Personal Collections.* Agawam, MA: Silver Street Media, 2012.

———. "Those Amazing Library Bindings." *New Library Scene* 15 (October 1996): 9–10.

Baird, Brian J., Jana Krentz, and Brad Schaffner. "Findings from the Condition Surveys Conducted by the University of Kansas Libraries." *College and Research Libraries* 58, no. 2 (March 1997): 115–26.

Bancroft, Audrey F., et al. "A Forward-Looking Library Use Survey: WSU Libraries in the 21st Century." *Journal of Academic Librarianship* 27, no. 3 (1998): 216–24.

Brennan, Mary Alice. *A Practical Guide to Preservation in School and Public Libraries*. Syracuse, NY: ERIC Clearinghouse on Information Resources, Syracuse University, 1990.

Brown, Meg. "Publishers Bindings and Libraries: An Analysis of Problems and Solutions." *New Library Scene* 15 (October 1996): 5–7.

Campbell, Sheila J., Mike Donnelly, and Mik Wisniewski. "A Measurement of Service." *Scottish Libraries* 50 (March/April 1995): 10–11.

Corrado, Edward M., and Heather Moulaison Sandy. *Digital Preservation for Libraries, Archives, and Museums*. 2nd ed. Lanham, MD: Rowman & Littlefield, 2017.

Cummins, Thompson Randolph. "Survey Research: A Library Management Tool." *Public Libraries* 27 (Winter 1988): 178–81.

Drewes, Jeanne M., and Julie A. Page, eds. *Promoting Preservation Awareness in Libraries*. Westport, CT: Greenwood, 1997.

Harvey, D. R. *The Preservation Management Handbook: A 21st-Century Guide for Libraries, Archives, and Museums*. Lanham, MD: Rowman & Littlefield, 2014.

Jones, Maggie (Margaret J.). *Preservation Management of Digital Materials: A Handbook*. London: The British Library for Resource, the Council for Museums, Archives and Libraries, 2001.

Kaplan, Robert S., and David P. Norton. *Translating Strategy into Action: The Balanced Scorecard*. Boston: Harvard Business School Press, 1996.

Lavender, Kenneth. *Book Repair: A How-to-Do-It Manual*. 2nd ed. New York: Neal-Schuman, 2001.

Lull, William P. *Conservation Environment Guidelines for Libraries and Archives*. Ottawa: Canadian Council of Archives, 1995.

Morrow, Carolyn Clark, and Carole Dyal. *Conservation Treatment Procedures: A Manual of Step-by-Step Procedures for the Maintenance and Repair of Library Materials*. 2nd ed. Littleton, CO: Libraries Unlimited, 1986.

Ogden, Sherelyn. *Preservation Planning: Guidelines for Writing a Long-Range Plan*. Washington, DC: Andover, MA: American Association of Museums, Northeast Document Conservation Center, 1997.

Pew Research Center. "Book Reading 2016." September 2016. Accessed July 20, 2017. http://www.pewinternet.org.

Reilly, James M., Douglas W. Nishimura, and Edward Zinn. *New Tools for Preservation*. Washington, DC: Commission on Preservation and Access, 1995.

Reynolds, Anne, Nancy Carlson Schrock, and Joanna Margaret. "Preservation: The Public Library Response; A Preservation Survey of the Public Library in Wellesley." *Library Journal* 114 (February 15, 1989): 128–32.

Index

About the Author

Brian J. Baird was raised on a dairy farm in Idaho and graduated with his BS and MLIS degrees from Brigham Young University. He served as a conservator and preservation librarian at Princeton University and the University of Kansas. He has also taught preservation courses at several universities and consulted widely on preservation issues. Baird worked in the private sector for several years providing preservation and library binding services to libraries across the United States before returning to academia at Brigham Young University. He has been active in researching and publishing about preservation issues.